ЕВГЕНІЙ БАРАТЫНСКІЙ

EVGENY BARATYNSKY

TWAYNE'S WORLD AUTHORS SERIES

A Survey of the World's Literature

Sylvia E. Bowman, Indiana University
GENERAL EDITOR

N. P. Vaslef, U.S. Air Force Academy
EDITOR

E. A. Baratynsky

(TWAS 202)

TWAYNE'S WORLD AUTHORS SERIES (TWAS)

The purpose of TWAS is to survey the major writers—novelists, dramatists, historians, poets, philosphers, and critics—of the nations of the world. Among the national literatures covered are those of Australia, Canada, China, Eastern Europe, France, Germany, Greece, Italy, Japan, Latin America, New Zealand, Poland, Russia, Scandinavia, Spain, and the African nations, as well as Hebrew, Yiddish, and Latin Classical literature. This survey is complemented by Twayne's United States Authors Series and English Authors Series.

The intent of each volume in these series is to present a critical-analytical study of the works of the writer; to include biographical and historical material that may be necessary for understanding, appreciation, and critical appraisal of the writer; and to present all material in clear, concise English —but not to vitiate the scholarly content of the work by doing so.

E. A. Baratynsky

By Benjamin Dees

University of Miami

Twayne Publishers, Inc.　　:　:　　New York

For my mother and father and Tuula

Contents

Preface

E VGENY Baratynsky is a name not likely to be encountered often today. It remains relatively unknown even to the average reader who may be familiar with Pushkin, Lermontov, or Tyutchev. Rarely does it appear in scholarly studies either, alongside these and other well-known names of nineteenth-century Russian poets. Yet Baratynsky is generally considered the greatest contempory of Pushkin in an age which was especially distinguished for its poetic achievements.

In the present book I have not endeavored to explore all the various aspects and problems offered by Baratynsky's poetry. I have attempted to present a study of his lyrical verse in its overall unity, as the work of a poet with fundamentally intellectualist perspectives, manifested in the constant positing of thesis and antithesis. The longer poems are seen essentially as efforts to broaden these perspectives, to assimilate the Romantic moods of Pushkin and Byron.

In examining Baratynsky's poetry from this point of view, I have used the methods of critical analysis which seemed most appropriate to me. These range from the biographical and thematic to the more formal techniques, concerned with image, symbol, and poetic structure. I have not, however, included more than passing references to Baratynsky's metrical practices.

In order to trace the persistent development of Baratynsky's basic device of opposition from his first poems to those written just before his death, I have adopted a chronological approach. Chapter One is a brief biographical sketch. Chapter Two treats the verse written between 1819 and 1827, in which the mutual antipathy of two opposing attitudes assumes a constant outward projection, becoming ultimately a clash between life and death. Chapter Three considers the longer works, most of which were written during the 1820's. In Chapter Four, which covers the lyrics up to 1835,

I have tried to show that the earlier antipathy is confined to what may be called a prosaic, dissension-ridden reality—which itself is opposed to a higher place of synthesis and harmony. Chapter Five deals with the irresolvable contradictions of *Twilight* and the last poems.

Baratynsky revised his poems frequently and extensively, especially during the earlier years of his creativity. I have relied exclusively on his final versions, as printed in his *Complete Poems (Polnoe sobranie stikhotvoreniy)*, Leningrad, 1957. All quotations from his verse and from the prefaces to "Eda" and "The Gypsy Girl" are taken from this source. All translations from both Russian and French are mine.

I have also used the authority of this edition in regard to dating of individual works; as it is impossible to assign precise dates to many of the poems, all dates used are to be understood as approximate and as close to accurate as circumstances allow. Moreover, I have accepted the spelling "Baratynsky" (rather than "Boratynsky") as the one used most often by the poet himself and by the majority of literary scholars and historians.

The first draft of this study was a doctoral dissertation submitted to the Department of Slavic Languages and Literatures at Princeton University in 1967. I would like to express my appreciation to my dissertation director, Professor Richard Burgi, and to Mme. Nina Berberova. I am indebted, as well, to my other professors on the Slavic faculty at Princeton. Finally, I am grateful for the Fulbright-Hayes Fellowship which enabled me to complete my research in Finland and the Soviet Union.

Benjamin Dees

University of Miami
Coral Gables, Florida

Chronology

1800 February 19. Evgeny Abramovich Baratynsky born in village of Mara, Tambov province.

1808 Family moves to Moscow.

1810 Baratynsky's father, Abram Andreevich, dies; mother returns to Mara with children.

1812 Baratynsky sent to German boarding school in Petersburg for six months of preparation prior to enrollment in Pages' Corps.

1816 Expelled from Pages' Corps for collaboration in theft; returns to the country.

1819 Enlists in army in Petersburg; first poems appear.

1820 Made non-commissioned officer, transferred to Finland.

1821 Joins Free Society of Lovers of Russian Literature.

1825 Promoted to lieutenant; lives in Moscow; retires from army.

1826 Marries Nastasia Lvovna Engelgardt, daughter of landowner; publishes "Eda, a Tale of Finland," and "Feasts, a Descriptive Poem" (Eda, finlyandskaya povest, and Piry, opisatelnaya poema).

1827 Publishes Poems of Evgeny Baratynsky (Stikhotvorenia Evgenia Baratynskogo); begins work in government land surveying office.

1828 Publishes "The Ball" (Bal); forms close friendship with Ivan Kireevsky.

1831 Publishes "The Gypsy Girl" (Tsyganka); retires from government service.

1835 Buys house in Moscow; publishes second collection of verse, Poems of Evgeny Baratynsky (Stikhotvorenia Evgenia Baratynskogo).

1836 Assumes management of Muranovo, one of Engelgardt estates near Moscow.

1840 Visits Petersburg; begins building house at Muranovo.

1842 Publishes last collection of verse, Twilight (Sumerki).

1843 Leaves with his wife and older children on trip to Western Europe.

1844 Dies on June 29; his body brought from Naples to Petersburg the next year, buried in Alexander Nevsky Monastery.

CHAPTER I

Biographical Background

Baratynsky, an austere and gloomy poet, who so soon displayed a
distinctive aspiration toward inner life in his thoughts and began
to fret about their exterior adornment, when they had not yet even
matured in him; obscure and undeveloped, he began to manifest himself to people and, accordingly, became alienated from everyone and
close to no one.[1]

I N this comment on the poetry of E. A. Baratynsky, Gogol expressed an opinion typical of the time—the middle forties of the
nineteenth century. The Golden Age of Russian poetry, whose
zenith had been reached in the 1820's, seemed remote. The mainstream of Russian literature was now preoccupied with new trends
in the directions of Realistic prose: the first works of Dostoevsky,
Goncharov, and Turgenev were to appear before 1850, and Tolstoy
was to write his first story two years later. Gogol's own masterpiece
in prose, *Dead Souls*, had appeared in 1842.

Poetry and the appreciation of poetry were entering a period of
decline. By the middle 1840's most of the poets associated with the
Golden Age had either disappeared from the scene or had with-
drawn into silence. Among those of the older generation, Batyushkov became mentally unbalanced in 1821; Katenin wrote little after
1832; Gnedich died in 1833, Davydov, in 1839, and Kozlov the following year; Zhukovsky settled in Germany after 1841.

Those of the younger generation similarly vanished from sight.
For participation in the Decembrist Uprising of 1825, Ryleev was
hanged, Bestuzhev and Kyukhelbeker suffered exile and imprison-
ment. The young Venevitinov died in 1827; Delvig, in 1831. Pushkin was killed in 1837 and, after prolonged ailments, Yazykov died in
1846. Alone of this group, Vyazemsky lived on until 1878, forgotten
and embittered.

I *Youth and "Exile"*

Baratynsky's lifetime traced the earliest beginnings and the conclusive ending of the first great age of Russian poetry. Historically, these years witnessed the reign of Alexander I and the Napoleonic Wars, the Decembrist Uprising, the Polish Revolt, and the repressions of Nicholas I.

Far from the noise and history-making activity of imperial Petersburg lay the small country estate of Mara where Baratynsky passed his first eight years. Here he learned French from Giacinto Borghese, a tradesman-turned-tutor, who, with his endless tales of Rome and the Colosseum, of Naples and Vesuvius, had somehow found his way into the isolation of Tambov. Apart from French, "Bubinka" (as the young Baratynsky was known in his family) showed an unusual interest in mathematics.

Later, in a Petersburg boarding school, the quiet, sensitive boy acquainted himself with seventeenth and eighteenth-century Classical French literature. The influence of his reading began to appear in the stilted, bookish letters in French he wrote to his mother during this time; for example:

> How I would like to be with you in the country now!...O, when will this happy moment arrive? Do I, in vain, hasten it by my prayers? Why, beloved Mama, have men devised the laws of convention which separate us? Would it not be better to be a happy simpleton than an unhappy scholar?[2]

The young student became so infatuated with his reading of French literature that he neglected his German, and upon entering the Pages' Corps, he was placed one class lower than was usual for his age. Meanwhile, the reflective, melancholy element in his personality did not diminish. At fourteen he wrote to his mother:

> We have just learned with the greatest regret of the death of our grandmother. I did not have the pleasure of knowing her, but if she was like you, how I should have loved her! I understand your grief, but think, beloved Mama, it is the law of nature. We are born in order to die, and a few hours sooner or later, we will have to depart this particle of mud called earth. We hope that in a better world, we can meet again those whom we have loved. God loves us, and He will not, to be sure, want to offer us an unhappy eternity after a life filled with so many adversities.[3]

Beginning in 1814 Baratynsky's behavior in the Corps started to fluctuate between good and bad. He grew dissatisfied and restless. Subsequently, he fell into bad company, and in February, 1816, he and his friends, taken up with Schiller's *Die Räuber*, formed a "society of avengers." The last and most serious of their pranks consisted in the theft of a gold snuff box containing 500 rubles. The theft was discovered, the culprits were identified, and two months later Baratynsky was expelled from the Corps and forbidden by the Emperor to serve in the army except as a private.

In a sense Baratynsky never completely recovered from this disgrace, and it found repeated expression in his poetry, especially during the first half of the 1820's. In May he left Petersburg to live on his uncle's estate in Smolensk, where he was to experience something of a nervous breakdown. In time the country helped him to recover—to an extent—from the shock, and he once again began to read a great deal, concentrating on the eighteenth-century Classical Russian writers and the Classical French poets.

As before, his reading stimulated his natural tendency toward reflection of an analytical and melancholy type; he wrote to his mother from Smolensk:

Such a man, in the midst of everything which appears to render him happy, endures a concealed venom, which torments him and renders him incapable of all perception of delight. A gloomy disposition, a depth of ennui and sadness—this is what he endures in the excitement of joy, and I know this man well.

Would not happiness be a certain combination of chance ideas, which renders us incapable of thinking of anything else except that which fills our heart, which would be filled so that it could not ponder on what it feels?. . . The passion for reasoning is not one of my smallest shortcomings, and I don't think to break myself of it.[4]

At the end of 1818 Baratynsky returned to Petersburg to enlist as a private in the army in the hope of redeeming his disgrace by promotion to the officers' ranks. In the capital an old friend of the Pages' Corps, Alexander Krenitsyn, introduced him to the poets of the Lycée circle, among them, Pushkin, Delvig, and Kyukhelbeker.

In February of the next year he became a soldier in the Household Troops and moved into an apartment with Delvig. Through Delvig, Baratynsky was introduced into the Petersburg literary salons, where he met Zhukovsky, Davydov, and Gnedich, among others. One of the most popular and lively of these salons belonged to Sofia Ponomaryova. The new associations with the best poets of Russia, the intimate friendship with Delvig, and the exposure to the congenial literary atmosphere of Petersburg all had a substantial effect on the nineteen-year-old Baratynsky and were instrumental in awakening the poet in him. Impressionable and perceptive, he began to write and Delvig published his first poems.

His stay in the capital was cut short in January, 1820, when he was made a noncommissioned officer. Shortly thereafter, he was suddenly transferred to Finland, which had been incorporated into the Empire following the conclusion of the Russo-Swedish War in 1809. Both Baratynsky and his friends were inclined to regard this transfer as exile (it coincided with Pushkin's banishment to the south of Russia), but his actual situation was better than that of many officers. He lived in the home of the regimental commander, Georgy Lutkovsky, who owned an estate in the same area of Tambov where Mara was located. Nikolay Konshin, his company commander and a minor poet, became one of his best friends.

The regiment moved about often and Baratynsky spent leaves and even tours of duty in Petersburg and Moscow. In 1822, for example, he was stationed for several months in Petersburg, where he resumed his earlier living arrangement with Delvig. Apart from these contacts, his friends frequently visited him in Finland.

In his verse during these years he created a picture of himself in solitude and isolation, surrounded only by the stern and rugged Finnish landscape. In fact, however, he remained an active participant in the Petersburg literary groups. The appearance of the elegy "Finland" (Finlyandia) and the longer "Feasts" (Piry) had already marked the beginning of a rising popularity. His circle of friendships broadened to include Bestuzhev and Ryleev, the publishers of the North Star (Polyarnaya zvezda), one of several periodicals in which fragments of his first long poem "Eda" were to appear.

In spite of his growing reputation, primarily as that of an elegiac poet, he continued to be distressed by his ambiguous social position. In the spring of 1824, when the regiment was inspected by General Arseny Zakrevsky, the Governor-General of Finland, the poet was pointed out to the general's adjutants, one of whom— Nikolay Putyata—was to become Baratynsky's close friend and brother-in-law. Putyata described his first impression: "I was walking in front of the formation behind General Zakrevsky...when Baratynsky was pointed out to me....He was then twenty-four. He was thin, pale, and his features expressed a profound dejection."[5]

In the autumn, through Putyata's mediation, Baratynsky was transferred to Zakrevsky's corps headquarters in Helsinki. Here he became infatuated with the general's wife, Agrafena Fyodorovna, a somewhat strange and interesting woman, whose emotional impulsiveness combined with a sharp intelligence. As before, however, passion coexisted in his personality with a cool and reasoning detachment, and it was characteristic of him to write to Putyata concerning Zakrevskaya: "I am hurrying to her; you will suspect that I'm a bit carried away. A bit, yes; but I hope, that the first hours of solitude will restore my reason. I'll write a few elegies and fall asleep peacefully."[6]

After his promotion the next year, which was achieved through the repeated efforts of Zhukovsky, Davydov, Vyazemsky, and others, Baratynsky left Finland for good. Marriage followed retirement from the army, and it seemed to him that he had entered a new period of stability and inner harmony.

II *Kireevsky*

Vyazemsky wrote Pushkin that Nastasia Engelgardt was "a polite girl, intelligent, and kind but not elegiac in appearance."[7] She became a gentle, if jealous wife, with a refined taste in poetry; Baratynsky often revised his poems according to her suggestions. In many ways he allowed himself to drift under the sway of a gratifying and solicitous domination, and he confided to Putyata that he had "exchanged the restless dreams of passions for the quiet dreams of a quiet happiness: instead of an actor, I have become a spectator...."[8]

But it proved to be only an outer shell of calm. Within him persisted the confusion and disorder that he had always known and, in a certain sense, would always know. He lived in contention with contradictions and with the unfailing tendency to reflect, to become entangled in inner dialectics from which there seemed to be no escape.

In Moscow Baratynsky gradually began to take part in a literary environment heretofore alien: he was accustomed to the traditions and friends of the Petersburg circles, but Pushkin and Vyazemsky were in Moscow, and through them, he was presented in the salons, including that of Zinaida Volkonskaya. Here among the habitual guests were the "Wisdom-lovers" *(Lyubomudry)*—young partisans of German philosophy and especially the idealistic teachings of Friedrich Schelling. Among others, they included Ivan Kireevsky,

Dmitry Venevitinov, Alexey Khomyakov, Stephan Shevyryov,
and Vladimir Odoevsky. At the same time Baratynsky met Yazykov
and Adam Mickiewicz.

In the spring of 1827 he went to Mara. His first collection of poems
appeared just before he returned to Moscow in November, and it
was greeted favorably by nearly all the critics. He subsequently
went to work for the government and served in the land surveying
office. During this time he lived in the Engelgardt home opposite
that of Vyazemsky on Chernyshevsky (today Stankevich) Street.

During the next few years Baratynsky moved about restlessly,
spending his time in Moscow and Mara and on the various estates
belonging to his wife's family. At the same time he was connected
with several publishing enterprises, including the *Moscow Tele-
graph (Moskovskiy telegraf),*to which Vyazemsky often contributed,
and Delvig's *Literary Gazette (Literaturnaya gazeta).*

More and more, however, he had begun to drift away from his
old friends and to show more interest in the activities and ideas
of the Wisdom-lovers, who had begun to disintegrate as a group.
Odoevsky went to Petersburg in 1826, Venevitinov died the following year, and Shevyryov went abroad in 1829. Kireevsky remained in Moscow until 1830, and it was with him—six years his
junior—that Baratynsky was to form an intimate friendship that was
to last some ten years.

In 1831 he wrote to Kireevsky from Kazan: "Of all the people I
know, you are the first, with whom I express my feelings without
reserve: this means, that no one up to now inspired me with such
trust in his soul and character."[9] This special relationship with Kireevsky was typical of a certain lack of single-mindedness in Baratynsky's nature and of his need to be close to those who had a
stronger will than he, and who could provide moral support for him.

This need had had disastrous consequences for him when he was
still a boy in the Pages' Corps. Now the results were constructive
and, under Kireevsky's influence, his literary activities intensified
and assumed a sense of direction, which had been wanting since his
arrival in Moscow from Petersburg and Finland. His reading was
now guided by Kireevsky—mostly Rousseau and Villemain, a pop-
ularizer of Schelling. During 1828 and 1829 Baratynsky participated
in the publication of the *Moscow Herald (Moskovskiy vestnik),*
with which Kireevsky was closely identified. In the meantime Romantic themes and motifs abstracted from Schelling had already
begun to appear in his poetry, even if he remained indiffierent to
the philosophical system as such.

In 1831 Delvig died; Pushkin wrote to Pyotr Pletnyov, one of the intimates of the Petersburg literary circles and a minor poet: "Without him we have become as if orphaned. Count on your fingers: how many of us are there? you, me, Baratynsky, that's all."[10] Actually, with the death of Delvig, the former group of Petersburg poets fell apart once and for all, as each became preoccupied with other interests and affairs. Their tastes and traditions and ideals were retiring from the foreground and with them was going the ascendency of poetry in Russian literature. Pushkin himself was turning to prose.

During these years Baratynsky's popularity began to suffer acutely. In attempting to adapt to current Romantic trends which demanded passionate, Byronic personalities, he had written the long poems "The Ball" (*Bal*) and "The Gypsy Girl" (*Tsyganka*). But the results of these essentially experimental ventures induced, as "Eda" had induced, a largely negative reaction from the reading public. The appearance of "The Gypsy Girl," especially, wrecked what little of his reputation was left.

In 1832 Baratynsky started working with Kireevsky's new periodical, the *European (Evropeets)*, which had set for itself the task of defending the so-called spiritual culture of Russia against the encroaching rationalistic and industrial culture of Western Europe. Based on Schelling's philosophy of history, according to which each nation had a special, predestined purpose—a specific contribution to make—this ideology saw Russia's mission as preserving and giving new life to the culture of the world.

Accordingly, Kireevsky and his colleagues identified historical progress with spiritual progress, and thus rejected contemporary European industrialization, a stage of development which Russia was to be spared. In order to transcend Europe, however, Russia must first graft onto its own backward culture all the spiritual enlightenment of the West—which had already reached its pinnacle of achievement in this sense—and then surpass it. The realization of this goal, in particular, was to be promoted by the *European*.

Baratynsky assimilated some of these ideas from a poetic standpoint and began writing, among other things, a drama for the *European*. However, the periodical was closed down by the regime of Nicholas I almost immediately after it began to appear. Baratynsky was overcome with gloom and wrote to Kireevsky from Kazan: "What, after this, can one attempt in literature? . . . What to do! We will reflect in silence. . . . We will write, but not publish. . . . Write to me. I need your letters."[11]

His depression did not abate. His popularity of the 1820's had all
but disintegrated; all the hopes and efforts he had put into the *European* were smashed; and he was experiencing moods of withdrawal and alienation. He generalized his feelings in another letter
to Kireevsky:

> The poetry of faith is not for us. We are so far from the sphere of the
> new reality, that we, indeed, do not comprehend it completely and feel
> it still less. We look at the European enthusiasts, almost as sober men
> look at drunks, and if their transports are sometimes comprehensible
> to our minds, they generally do not appeal to our hearts. What for
> them is actuality, for us is abstraction. Subjective poetry alone is natur-
> al for us. Egoism is our legitimate godhead, as we have dethroned old
> idols and have not yet come to believe in new ones.[12]

In general the background of this letter was the July Revolution
in France; more specifically, it was the collection of poems (*Iambes*)
by Henri Barbier dedicated to the Revolution. As indicated in his
letter, the activities of the European revolutionaries failed to arouse
a deep response in Baratynsky. Although he had been close to several of the Decembrists, he had never been of an actively political
turn of mind.

Meanwhile he was preparing a second collection of his poems
for publication, and wrote Vyazemsky that nothing would follow it.
As a further token of his growing disillusionment, he asserted that
"the time of subjective poetry has passed," and that the time for
a new kind of poetry had not yet come.[13]

In 1833 he met Pushkin by chance in Kazan, when the latter was
on his way to collect materials for his history of the Pugachyov Rebellion. Back in Moscow, Baratynsky began to help Kireevsky and
the collaborators of the *Moscow Herald* to organize a new periodical,
the *Moscow Observer (Moskovskiy nablyudatel)*.

In the beginning, this periodical advocated the same line of
thought as the *European*: negation of mercantilism and, accordingly, respect for past European culture, but pessimism in regard to its
future. When the first number appeared in March of 1835, Baratynsky's "The Last Poet" *(Posledniy poet)* followed Shevyryov's
lead article, "Literature and Commerce" *(Slovesnost i torgov-
lya)*. As had both the *Moscow Herald* and the *European*, the *Observer*, too, found its roots in Schelling's philosophy; however, it was
now an ideology based in a later Schelling, who in his older years
was involved in religion and mystical revelation.

Baratynsky, absorbed in estate duties, published nothing in the *Observer* after 1835. His second collection of poems, published in that year, had no success whatsoever. The following year the first of Pyotr Chaadaev's controversial "Philosophical Letters" *(Filosoficheskie pisma)* appeared; he had been an intimate of the *Observer* circle, and now the journal was subjected to a censorship which stripped it of most of its meaning. Pushkin was killed in 1837. A new literary generation was arising in Moscow, epitomized by Belinsky and his associates, and they were turning to Hegel, who stressed reason and logic at the expense of Schelling's nature-philosophy and esthetic perception.

In the spring of 1838 the *Observer* was taken over by Belinsky and Bakunin, and it soon folded. Meanwhile Kireevsky, Khomyakov, and Shevyryov were undergoing a further evolution in the direction of Orthodoxy and Slavophilism. Baratynsky did not follow them and his relationship with them began to suffer accordingly. More and more he found himself in frustrated isolation.

III *Disjunction*

All of these events could not but affect Baratynsky in a deeply personal way. He was now virtually alone. Delvig and Pushkin, his two main links with the 1820's, were gone. His long friendship with Kireevsky was wearing thin, and his participation in Kireevsky's circle diminished. Because he stood on the side lines in the incipient Slavophil-Westernizer debates, he was ignored. The years were passing; he had been rejected and could expect nothing from the future.

In the beginning of 1839 he wrote to his old Petersburg friend Pletnyov: "These last ten years of existence, at first glance not having any distinction at all, were more agonizing for me than all the years of my seclusion in Finland. I am tired, I have lapsed into dejection."[14] He began to close himself off at Muranovo with his family and rumors spread of his heavy drinking.

During his visit to Petersburg in 1840, his first in fifteen years, Baratynsky saw many of his old friends, including Zhukovsky, Vyazemsky, Putyata, and Pletnyov. He also met Lermontov. His impressions were so vivid that he returned to Moscow with the intention of moving to Petersburg as soon as possible.

In the interim his break with Kireevsky's circle became more definite. Toward the beginning of the 1840's Kireevsky and his intimates began to publish an openly Slavophil periodical, the *Musco-*

vite (Moskvityanin), but Baratynsky had no part in it. Moreover, in the ensuing polemics between the *Muscovite* and Belinsky, he kept silent. Declining to take either side, he was distrusted by both. In the intrigues against Belinsky by Shevyryov and his colleagues, he suspected intrigues against himself as well. He was now finally cut off from the literary life of Moscow and alienated from the main currents of its artistic traditions and convictions.

In 1842 his last small collection of verse, *Twilight (Sumerki)*, was published. It provoked little reaction, and a contemporary was later to write: "When in 1842 Baratynsky's little book 'Twilight' came out, it produced the impression of an apparition, which appeared in the midst of amazed and perplexed people, not able to comprehend what kind of ghost it was and what it wanted from its descendants!"[15] Baratynsky buried himself with activities at Muranovo, where he and his family lived in complete solitude.

His spirits rose considerably during the long-desired trip to Western Europe the next year. Upon returning, he intended to settle in Petersburg. In September he set off with his wife and older children, arriving in Paris in November, where they remained for the winter. Here he became acquainted with many of the prominent French writers, including de Vigny, Mérimée, and Nodier. More interesting and important for him, however, was the success he enjoyed in the Russian emigré circles.

From France the family sailed to Naples in the spring of 1844, planning to visit Rome and Florence and to return to Russia in the autumn. But Baratynsky died suddenly in Naples on a morning late in June. His death caused little stir in the Russian literary press. A year later the body was brought to Petersburg and buried in the Alexander Nevsky Monastery.

CHAPTER 2

The Appeal to Reason

B ARATYNSKY'S arrival in Petersburg in the autumn of 1818 and his subsequent introduction to its literary life and atmosphere coincided with the real beginning of his own poetic activity. He quickly became an intimate in that diversified group of poets which came to be known variously as the "Pushkin Pleiad," the "Pushkin Circle," or simply as the "Poets' Circle."

The unity of this group, such as it was, was grounded in both social and literary factors. By birth these poets were aristocrats and thus could muster a solid front against the pedestrian journalists of the literary press—a vocation in which they themselves were not too successful. The literary components of their unity were less definite, yet nonetheless real; these were in the areas of tradition, nobility of poetic outlook, and overall attitude toward poetry. Characteristic of all of them was a refined sense of taste in poetic technique, embodied in elegant harmony, Classical restraint, and finished versification. More specifically, their common tendencies in language, style, and genre can be immediately traced to the Arzamas.

I Literary Influences

The Arzamas Society had been formed in 1815 by writers of a generation somewhat younger than Karamzin's and somewhat older than Pushkin's, who were, in general, advocates of Karamzin's literary and language innovations. The most important of the Arzamas poets were Zhukovsky, Batyushkov, Vyazemsky, and the young Pushkin. The society began to disintegrate in 1818, and with it disintegrated the more extreme manifestations of Karamzin's estheticism, mannerism, and stylistics.[1]

By this time, however, the essence of Karamzin's work was being affirmed in Russian poetry. He had rejected the elevated genres of French Classicism—the epic, ode, and tragedy—and replaced them by the *poésie légère* of the same Classicism, which included,

among others, the elegy, friendly epistle, epigram, madrigal, and
occasional verse. With the elevated genres went the solemn and
oratorical language in which they were written. The Karamzinian
poets modeled their use of Russian on the precise, refined medium
of expression which was characteristic of the French salon world
and also of *poésie légère*. In attempting to Europeanize the language, it was common practice to use smaller genres as material
for introducing and developing stylistic devices and novelties.

Most of the Petersburg poets in the early 1820's were connected,
to a greater or lesser degree, by these traditions—French Classical,
in origin. On the other hand, the question of Romanticism in the
European sense was scarcely relevant here, even if these poets were
attracted by Romantic themes. The majority were more Classical
in poetic temperament and form than perhaps they themselves
suspected, and they tended to avoid Romantic excesses and
ecstasies.

Scattered in their lyrics were allusions to Roman and Greek deities
and other diverse personalities from Classical mythology and culture, together with conventional Church Slavonicisms, and use of
vivid epithets and attributives. Epicurean themes of the delights
of youth, love, and the bottle coexisted with a melancholy taken
up with the untimely passing away of everything earthly. The cult
of friendship and art merged with the belief in the worth of the
indidivual and in freedom and independence of thought. The
elegy reached the peak of its popularity.

Baratynsky, with his own background in both Classical French
literature and philosophy and its reflection in the eighteenth-century
Russian writers, could not but feel a strong affinity with the Petersburg poets. Whereas the new impressions of the capital—his friendships with Delvig and Pushkin, the reading of Batyushkov and
Zhukovsky, and continual exposure to the literary salons—all had a
part in inspiring him to write, his actual poetic talent was developed
under the direct influence of the French authors, including Voltaire
(1694-1778), Casimir Delavigne (1793-1843), Jean François La
Harpe (1739-1803), and especially, the elegiac poets, Evariste
Parny (1753-1814), André de Chénier (1762-1794), Charles Hubert
Millevoye (1782-1816), and Charles Auguste La Fare (1644-1712).[2]
He absorbed the spirit and form of their verse, imitated it, and
translated it. He was never really to shake off the influence of his
early reading; his inclination toward reflective analysis was
first encouraged and then sustained by French rationalism.

Batyushkov was the Russian poet, perhaps, from whom he learned the most, but Batyushkov himself was strongly influenced by the same French poets that Baratynsky had known even as a youth. Batyushkov, together with Zhukovsky, had been among the first to adapt the Russian poetic language to the expression of tender, lyrical emotion. And not only Baratynsky, but most of the poets of the Petersburg circles in the early 1820's, employed Batyushkov's techniques, including his semantics, melodics, and his conventional motifs.

The influence of Zhukovsky is also perceptible in Baratynsky's early work, especially his elegies, but here the question is more one of assimilating a certain sensitivity of feelings and melancholy than anything else; Baratynsky tended to avoid Zhukovsky's mystical orientation. On a more personal level, Delvig, and to a lesser extent, Pushkin helped and encouraged the young Baratynsky—still somewhat intimidated by the incident at the Pages' Corps, to find and express himself in poetry.

His first poems were little more than stylistic exercises and are easily classified according to the various genres of *poésie légère*. His first elegies presented the traditional picture of a disillusioned youth, whose "spring" of life has passed irrevocably, and who is overcome with premature gloom. Commonplace metaphors and turns of speech abound. Much of this work shows the marked influence of Batyushkov; however, even in his earliest verse, Baratynsky eschewed Batyushkov's sensuality and smooth, flowing descriptiveness.

In a thematic sense this early verse was centered around the conflict of reason versus spontaneous happiness and emotion. Such a theme was not new in Russian poetry and had been, for example, already developed by Batyushkov. Indeed, such an opposition was symptomatic of the times in Russia, when the opposing principles of rationalistically-minded Classicism and the spontaneity of Romanticism, while heatedly debated in literary journals and newspapers, were merging in Russian poetry. What makes this preoccupation remarkable in Baratynsky is its very persistence, which can be traced, on one level or another, both in his personal letters and from his first poems to the works written just before his death.

Moreover, it is important to emphasize that Baratynsky's inclination to juxtapose these opposing principles and others more or less related to them was not the result of the direct influence of Batyush-

kov or of any other single figure, Russian or French. Rather, it was
the result of his education, of the times in which he lived, and of his
own particular personality, as poet and man.

On the other hand, an instance of the way in which Batyushkov's
influence may be seen in his early verse is demonstrated in the
simple and extended use of anaphora, as in "To °°°° on His Departure for the Army" *(K°°°° pri otezde v armiyu)*, 1820:

> I love the military tents,
> I love regimental carelessness,
> I love the beautiful parades,
> I love the battle apprehension,
> I love the valiant, soldier mine,
> I love to watch them. . . . (55)

Similar instances are numerous in Batyushkov's poetry; "To Nikita"
(K Nikite), 1817, is related in its theme to Baratynsky's epistle:
"They pass in terrifying silence! / They pass—with weapons all
atilt; / They pass...hurrah!...."[3] In later lyrics Baratynsky was to
apply this device in a far more sophisticated and original manner.

He substituted the plastic expressiveness of Batyushkov with a
more restrained and subtle development. His melancholy, conventional and Byronic in many respects, strikes a more sincere and
individual tone. At the same time, in his best and most characteristic elegies, it is hardly a subjective melancholy, but is refined and
formalized to the point of abstraction; these elegies began to
appear in the Petersburg journals of 1820.

II *The Elegies* (I)

Baratynsky was known, above all, for his elegies in the beginning
of the 1820's, and in a certain sense, while enriching and broadening
the elegiac canons of the time, he never moved completely beyond
these canons. Elegiacal moods of meditation and melancholy form a
continuous line in his work and are perceptible even in the majority
of his last poems. This section will deal with those of his elegies
which are inspired by a romantic addressee.

"The Complaint" *(Ropot)*, 1820, is a typical example of his calm
melancholy, mirrored in the quietness of an "afflicted soul,"
incapable of experiencing rapture at the thought of an approaching
rendezvous. The mood is one of renunciation, underlined by an
almost complete lack of passion. Such a mood in the romantic

elegy of the early 1820's constituted a departure from tradition; here the disillusioned youth is suffering not from unpleasant or unacceptable circumstances in his romantic life, but from the incapacity to love. This situation was later to become common in Russian poetry, but it was first introduced by Baratynsky and Pushkin.[4]

The perplexed psychological state of the lyrical hero is implicit in the pointed conclusion: "It seems I'm happy to mistake,/ And gladness doesn't suit me" (55). Reflected here is an expression of the divided personality of the boy in his letters to his mother, whose "concealed venom"—the "passion for reasoning" and cool analysis of his own emotions—destroys his possibility for happiness.

A similar perplexity pervades "The Parting" (*Razluka*), 1820. This elegy is thematically close to Parny's "Que le bonheur arrive lentement," which had been translated by Batyushkov (1804 or 1805). However, Baratynsky's essentially analytical version bears little resemblance to either Parny or Batyushkov.

Unlike the preceding poem, "The Parting" explores the psychological reaction to loss of a transient happiness through contrast of that "brief moment" in the past with the disenchantment of the present. Accentuating this contrast are both constant changes in verbal tense, which highlight the stages of past joys, present disillusionment, and a resolve "not to love" in the future, and recurrent terminology—especially effective when identical words are repeated in opposite contexts (i.e., *Ya vsyó imél, lishílsya vdrúg vsegó*) ("I had everything, suddenly was deprived of all") (56). Sharply focused is the disappointed bewilderment of the lyrical hero, who ponders on the discrepancy between short-lived delight and the "despondent confusion" which remains.

Connected to each of these elegies in its tranquil mood of weariness and inconsolability, its lack of apparent subjectivity, is "Dissuasion" (*Razuverenie*), 1821; it transcends, however, the confusion felt earlier. Its air of renunciation is augmented by negatives, which occur in eight lines out of sixteen. There is not even a suggestion of emotion in the disillusionment of the poet: his passion belongs to the past, and he recalls it calmly, wrapped in an inner world of indifference and impotence that nothing can disturb. The overtones of incapability of love in "The Complaint" and the decision not to "breathe the breath of love" in "The Parting" receive more pronounced expression.

Another tendency in "The Complaint," that of near lack of

imagery, is carried to the point of complete lack of visible imagery.[5]
The over-all "visual" effect is one of translucence and emptiness,
which harmonizes with the vacuity of the soul. Only the gentle,
unhurried motion of the rhythm, realized in the exceptional, but
balanced, recurrence of pyrrhics, assists in conveying impressions
given by semantics. The refusal to "believe in love" further emphasizes the cool and detached rationality felt throughout.

Heightening this psychological effect is the careful selection of
attributives. In the elegiac language developed by Zhukovsky and
Batyuskov, epithets tended to become traditional[6] and obli-
gatory, and eventually led to a sense of monotony. By choosing
strikingly original epithets, Baratynsky infused new shades of
meaning into his best elegies,[7] which reflected the correspondingly
new psychological content. Thus, the "solicitous friend" (*drug
zabotlivyy*) in "Dissuasion" acquires feelings heretofore undeveloped in the elegy of the early 1820's.

The poet drowses here, suspended in an immobile languor; the
concluding quatrain, appearing after an extended series of nega-
tively-inspired imperatives, represents the logical end result of this
emotional impassivity:

> I sleep, and this repose is sweet;
> Forget the fantasies that were:
> Within my soul you will awaken
> Excitement only—but not love. (70)

This concrete, psychologically-individualized attitude distinguished
Baratynsky's romantic elegies from those of the other Petersburg
poets, in particular, from those of Delvig, who was interested in a
picturesque and generalized treatment.

"To...O" (*K...O*), 1821, addressed to Ponomaryova, is more
specific in pinpointing psychological motivations of aloofness
and withdrawal in this poetic mentality: "With the allure of charming speeches / You'll not deprive me of my reason!" (78). The poet
is thus attempting to preserve his reason at the expense of the
irrational qualities of love. The mutual opposition of "me" to
"you" in these introductory lines is one that occurs throughout
the first three stanzas. Such a systematically consistent unfolding
of lyrical subject matter creates the effect of a sustained collision
between prudence and passion; in this regard the addressee
functions as a metaphor for passion.

In the last stanza he retires from the field without doing battle.

Reason thus gains the upper hand once more, as it does in another poem to Ponomaryova, "In the Album" (*V albom*), 1822, where the reasoning faculty is identified as a "secret voice."

In none of the previous elegies does the image of the addressee attain visual features. The lyrical hero is more interested in giving expression to his own state of mind than in drawing a picture of the beloved, the lack of which heightens the abstract atmosphere and psychological tonalities of these poems. Certain specifics about her are clear, however, and the most obvious is her infidelity.

"To Deliya" (*Delii*), 1822, again addressed to Ponomaryova, constitutes an infrequent exception to the absence of concrete detail in connection with the person of the beloved. Interestingly enough, the poet prefers to visualize the future Deliya—one with whom the logical progression of time has already had its way.

Here Baratynsky, in a typically rationalistic mood, sets forth the destiny of an unfeeling temptress surrounded by admirers, a theme traditional in eighteenth-century French erotic poetry. Deliya, however, is addressed in dry, ironic tones devoid of any suggestion of conventional lyrical intimacy or elegiac emotion. The examination of her bleak prospects is pursued with merciless persistence and stark, realistic clarity:

> With artistry you will round out your withered breast,
>   You'll paint your haggard cheeks with red,
> The little god of love you'll want in every way
>   To charm once more... but you'll not charm!
> In return for youthful dreams it's not for you to find
>   The peace, solace of older years.... (85)

The contrast between her impassioned present and a future spent in vain attempts to lure Cupid is pointed up by the repetition of "charm" (*primanit*) in the same line. "Peace" is also given a sharp semantic contour by its carry-over in the enjambment; this "peace" is understood to be at variance with the fleeting "peace" which Deliya now enjoys. The subsequent portrayal of an aged and bitter coquette, attended by constant explosions of "imperious provocations," is drawn in the same pungent outlines.

These considerations are terminated by a comparison, underscored by telling juxtaposition of opposites:

> One not at peace within on the peaceful couch of sleep
>   Untroubled resting thus abandons,
> And where for everyone tranquility is easy,
>   Turmoil alone awaits its victim. (85)

A general psychological significance is thus given to Deliya's experience. And by arriving at this generalization, the poet has employed a reasoning almost mathematical in its method; by proving that something is true of a particular case, he aspires to prove that it will be true of any case in that series. He infers a general concept from particular circumstances. He invests an emotional motif with logical implications. In its cold consistency of thought, expressed in weighted, solemn tones, and in its complete lack of subjectivity, the poem transcends the limits of the traditional romantic elegy as it was known in the early 1820's.

"The Kiss" (*Potseluy*), 1822, forms a sharp contrast to "To Deliya," as it effects a reversal in approach and mood; but as before, happiness is beyond the poet's reach. This lyric is based on a single sensual detail, which acquires the dimensions of an entire emotional response. The unforgettable impression of a kiss merges into the "you" and the "delight" of a dream; in turn, the dream unfolds into the sentiment of reality, combining love and the anguish of love, both of which are subtly embodied in the kiss and the memory of the kiss. A circle is thus described, which, beginning with reality, traverses a dream to return to reality—through all of which the image and the moment of the kiss remain fixed. Herein lies the inner contradiction mirrored in the complexity of the sentiment, which combines love and the "enervation" (*iznemozhenie*) of love: the momentary aspect of the kiss itself as opposed to its ever-present duration in the memory.

The absence of happiness is emphasized both by interruption of the evenly-flowing rhythm in line seven, where a nonmetrical stress on "no" occurs, and by the position of the exclamation ("no happiness!"), isolated by punctuation in the center of the line: *Obman ischez, net schastya! i so mnoy...* (-/-///---/) ("The deception has disappeared, there is no happiness! and with me...") (86). Technical unity is imposed by syntactic parallels, euphonic accord, and the rhyme pattern, which consists of one simple alternation in all of the eight lines. Line five may be singled out for its special harmony and balance, apparent in the constant stress of the same sound and the even positioning of the particle *li: Soydyót li són i vzór somknyót li móy*—("Will sleep come and close my eyes—") (86).

Many of Baratynsky's elegies and lyrics are bound together in an evident elegiac cycle, characteristic of Classical poetic practices of the end of the eighteenth and the beginning of the nineteenth centuries,⁵ in which one or the other poem embodies a specific mood or attitude. "Discord" (*Razmolvka*), 1823, with its subdued and sensitive tonality, delicate texture and near lack of visual imagery has affinities with "The Complaint," "The Parting," "Dissuasion," and "The Kiss." It reveals, as do the other poems, a typically analytical development, both thematically and formally.

The opposition between the two parties noted in "To...O" is tempered by lassitude and a stronger dose of resignation. This condition is emphasized by the lack of verbs of action in reference to the lyrical hero:

> You used to speak to me of love in jest
> And coldly now you may confess to this.
> I've recovered; no, no, I'm not a child!
> Forgive me, I now know the world myself. (92)

In the concluding quatrain the incident takes on an aura at once impersonal and impassive, which is reflected in the reasoned posing and resolving of questions. In the last line, however, the poet's passive qualities lose their straightforwardness and acquire a second dimension in the admission of the possibility of past love on his part. It is in this tenderly unresolved note, carrying a suggestion of feeling, that is capsuled Baratynsky's ability to grasp and convey the most refined nuance of emotion and to fix it firmly, to eternize it without the aid of perceptible imagery.

"The Confession" (*Priznanie*), 1823, belongs to the same elegiac cycle as "Discord"; but whereas the latter and the short elegies, when taken together, appear as impressionistic episodes of a more extended record, "The Confession," with its more elaborate elements of composition, presents a completeness in itself. It becomes a focal point in a lyrical history of romantic feelings, toward which the others gravitate, assuming more definite outlines in the process.

Written in six, five, and four-foot iambic lines, this elegy tells of a disillusionment begot by dried-up inner resources, by incapacity to be swayed either by passion or memories of passion. The metrically shorter lines add brittle notes of finality to this outlook and tend to function as lesser climaxes. A light melancholy pervades the opening lines, as the lyrical hero begins his internal monologue of apathy with a characteristic negative expression: "Pretended tenderness do not demand of me,/ The pensive coldness of my heart I won't conceal" (100).

In more detail than in any of the previous elegies he investigates the causes for his detached state of imperturbability. Psychological restlessness and turbulence have left an indelible imprint on the soul and there is no hint of its former agitations: the vital motion of the past has frozen into "lifeless recollections." In this gradual recession of feelings, the possibility of love has been extinguished, and he regrets the process which has left an inevitable layer of impotence in its wake. The intention not to love again, noted in "The Parting" as a youthful reaction to infidelity, is here but one of several confirmations in a confession of over-all incapacity.

Seldom has resignation in the face of "destiny" been expressed so serenely. The prospect of a future which includes the probability of marriage without love is pursued with the same disarming calm. Unable to give himself to love, he will nevertheless submit to a carefully deliberated union characterized by the absence of "emotional whims." Moreover, the ensuing sorrow is to be pacified by "reason."

The concluding lines take the form of an inductive generalization, reminiscent of "To Deliya":

> We're powerless in our own selves
> And, in our youthful years
> We utter hasty promises,
> Ridiculous, perhaps, to all-seeing fate. (101)

There is little of traditional elegiacal disillusionment or Byronic alienation here; rather, the elegy is concerned with methodical and introspective analysis of an individual mentality involved with the contradictory concepts of emotion and impassive rationality. It is the rational principle which gains ascendancy, but its apparent victory is incomplete, as it must yet do battle with the "unavailing sorrow" which it induces.

In another of Baratynsky's elegies of the same period, "Vindication" (*Opravdanie*), 1824, the theme of mutual injustice is developed. The poet's infidelity unfolds in light tones of plastic expressiveness which recall Batyushkov.[9] In the continuation of these almost playful admissions, the setting shifts to ballroom dances, where the "strings" of the poetic lyre merge with the "strings" of the musical instruments. Here Baratynsky slips into an enumeration of passionately graphic details not typical of his lyric verse, in which the effect of movement is assisted by repeated instances of enjambment. Significantly, the image of the addressee is left in

shadows, and, as before, the lyrical hero is more concerned with
dealing with the features of his own response to romance. The
transience and light-mindedness of his ball-room pursuits are vindi-
cated in graceful mythological metaphors.

At this point the chain of avowals is broken and the straight-lined
psychological tonality becomes complicated by a shift of emphasis.
In a manner resembling that of the poems addressed to Ponomaryova, both parties become diametrically opposed to each other, and
two attitudes combine into one complex sentiment:

> No! more supercilious than tender,
> You still are laden with your own offenses...
> Goodbye forever!... (104)

In the concluding lines, recurrent terminology and a final allusion
to poetry function to join thematic levels, giving the elegy as a
whole the effect of a musical composition, in which one motif
evolves into another to achieve synchronization in the end. Corresponding to this device is another, wherein various motifs assume
the form of musical interludes played by the poet on his lyre.

Two other romantic elegies, "O capricious Sofia!" (*O svoenra-
vnaya Sofia!*), 1823, and "To..." (*k...*), 1824, of the same period
are permeated with the collision between passion and reason. In
the second of these, the poet wavers throughout from one to the
other, first conceding, for example, that he is "full of impassioned
anguish," and in the next line, refusing to forget his "reason."

The cult of precise form is felt in "Reassurance" (*Uverenie*),
1824; its theme and atmosphere of calm melancholy tie it to the
cycle of elegies centered in "The Confession." Even division into
statement (first sentence—quatrain) and development of statement
into metaphor (last sentence—quatrain) suggests a refined predilection for symmetry and balance. Characteristic, as well, of
Baratynsky's penchant for contrast is the transition from an impassioned lover to a quavering Old Believer, a transition nevertheless
built methodically by vocabulary: "incense," "shrine," "icon."
Preference for the beloved, as opposed to "others," is underscored
by constant repetition of the second person pronoun.

The analytical frame of mind reflected in the above poem finds
another expression in "Anticipation" (*Ozhidanie*), 1825, a translation of Parny's "Refléxion amoreuse." In contrast to the beginning, which is an emotional expectation, the conclusion constitutes

an exercise of the intellect, which endeavors to curb the rising
feeling.

The conflict between two attitudes, two modes of thinking,
is not resolved in Baratynsky's romantic elegies. If the atmosphere
of these elegies is frequently one of self-composure and detachment,
and if reason often proves to be the ascendant principle, there is no
real resolution of the two opposing concepts. The negative concept, the appeal to reason, is embodied in motifs of renunciation
and resignation, which are carefully supported by a rationalistic
bent.

Many of the elegies, in which a logical development of theme is
obvious, are accorded extra-logical features evident in syntactic
disposition and general principles of construction. In "The
Parting," for example, the impression is that cool, analytical structure functions as a balance to restrained feeling, acts as a psychological defense for romantic sensitivity and passion—the other
element of the conflict. In others, for instance, "Discord," rationalistic and Classical inclinations are subtly reflected both in structure
and in the constrained manner of the conclusion. However, despite
the meticulous building-up of motivations of rational indifference,
most notably in "The Confession," it fails to succeed in concealing
the emotional tension and sentiment lying beneath the surface.

III *The Elegies* (II)

The struggle between two opposing standards is continued in
this group of elegies and is expressed on various levels, apart from
the romantic. Typically, these poems tend to transcend the genre
of the traditional elegy in their abstract precision, rhetorical tonality,
and elevated vocabulary, but are distinguished by the same irresolution common to Baratynsky's romantic polemics.

An effort to identify and rationalize the basic elements of opposition is made in the naïve "Imitation of LaFare" (*Podrazhanie
Lafaru*), 1820, a free adaptation of the latter's "A madame la com-
tesse de Caylus." A new note follows the well-worn statement concerning the evanescence and deceit of hope:

> Instructed by the cheerless truth,
> Henceforward with an empty soul
> The lambent swarm of living joys
> I'll substitute with cold reflection
> And deathly silence of the heart! (57)

Truth is connected with cold reflection, from which ensues a silenced heart. There is no suggestion of a compromise, no mutual concession: the "lambent swarm of living joys" is in total contrast to the "empty soul," which truth demands as its price for inner tranquility. The concluding epicurean motif does not substantially lighten the impression created by the perception of this "cheerless truth."

In early 1820 Baratynsky was transferred to the lonely fortress of Kyumen in southeastern Finland, and "Finland" (*Finlyandia*), 1820, was one of his first poems to portray the austere Finnish landscape. Batyushkov, in his *Picture of Finland; a Fragment from the Letters of a Russian Officer (Kartina Finlyandii; otryvok iz pisem russkogo ofitsera)* of 1809, had also been fascinated with the Finnish countryside, but in Baratynsky's poetry, the lot of the poet "wandering in solitary melancholy" was to find a symbolic correspondence in the dismal nature of the North.

Finnish landscape, with its rocks, lakes, and forests, is treated extensively in "Finland." In the introductory lines the youthful and lighthearted poet with his lyre stands out against a backdrop of cliffs, silent and cold in their eternity. The subsequent realistic account of landscape and northern nightfall becomes an elegiac meditation on the ephemeral existence of heroes long since perished: the flames of their ceremonial blazing oak have "died away" (*ugas*) and proved to be no more lasting than the day, which has itself "died away" (*pogas*). Only the barren rocks remain as reminders of their turbulent existence, and in contrast to the noise and commotion of the past, these are now plunged into "profound silence." These lyrical reflections then concentrate on the present, and the poet reasons: "For all there is one law, the law of annihilation" (63).

"Finland" is a poem about time, both in its transience (represented by the departed heroes) and its eternity (the rocks). The poet, however, is both of these: "Not being eternal for ages, I'm eternal for myself" (63); his lyrical personality combines both the one concept and its opposite number. Accordingly, two conflicting entities join in one fixed framework: abstract movement (transience) is paired with abstract immobility (eternity). Completing this circle of thoughts is an art-for-art motif.

"To Delvig" (*Delvigu*), 1821, like "Finland," projects personal experience into a universal framework, a technique characteristic of so much of Baratynsky's later poetry. The first of his six poems in blank verse, it is written in the spirit of the philosophical ode of the eighteenth century, and its solemn overtones and archaic terminology are at odds with Baratynsky's Karamzinist orientation.

Here the impossibility of happiness, treated in mythological terms, is presented as a direct result of mankind's origin: the "earthly children of Prometheus" have been denied that celestial state and are condemned to an "allotted term" of illness and suffering before death.   Corresponding to the mythological setting and adding a pronounced note of determinism is the Classical motif of "inexorable fate."

The opposition between "heavenly" and "earthly" in the first stanza is echoed by that between "life" and "death" in the third. The element of unity is again the poetic personality, encompassing contrasting phenomena in the range of its experience. Contradiction is given especially pointed expression in the third stanza: "To love and to cherish the illness of life, / And be frightened of comforting death" (71). Euphony in these lines (and others) in the original tends to neutralize, in part, the emotional intensity underlying the development of poetic thought: Lyu*bít i* lelé*yat* ne*dúg bytiá/ I* smér*ti otrá*dnoy* stra*shítsya* (71).

The central contradiction, manifested in the paradoxical character of human nature, is set forth in stanza five:

> But we received life in the heavenly spark,
> Our heavenly home we remember,
> In longing for happiness ever towards it
> We strive with indefinite longing!...(71)

Earthly man is unable to forget the divine spark of Prometheus, which gives him a link to heaven. And because of his duality, he is caught spiritually between heaven and earth, not belonging entirely to either. He can only stand rejected on the earth, as punished Prometheus hung chained to his cliff, and gaze helplessly at the "triumphal arch" of the skies—the embodiment of a happiness he can yearn for, but never know.

This essentially Romanticist conception of man as an exile and the attendant dream of a celestial homeland merge with an atmosphere and style inspired by Classicism.   In the last stanza the image of Prometheus is replaced by that of Tantalus being consumed by thirst in a pool of cool water—another symbol of mankind and the proximity, but inaccessibility, of heaven.

The elegy "Rome" (*Rim*), 1821, goes back to Baratynsky's long-standing interest in Classical Italy. Concrete images are refined to abstractness here and tend to disappear in a generality for which they provide but a context. Transience and instability are symbolized by the silent ruins of a once-powerful imperial capital, now forgotten by the gods. Its antiquity is enveloped in an austere and solemn framework and intensified by use of Church Slavonic words.

Moreover, the very existence of ancient Rome is called into question in the first stanza: "Did you exist, proud Rome, dictator of the earth, / Did you exist, O sovereign Rome?" (76). Built on a string of rhetorical questions, the verse texture, as distinct from the imagery, acquires an impression both of solidity and substantiality, enhanced by the comparative infrequency of verbs.

Highlighting the ethereal atmosphere in this vision is the sweeping depiction in the third stanza, where the city, as if suspended in a timeless moment stands on the "crossroads of the ages" like a "grand sarcophagus of perished generations." Impermanence is thus augmented by an allusion to death. The contrast between past and present receives its ultimate development in the last stanza, where Rome is reduced to an "apparition-accuser" sadly presenting its lived-out glory to the eyes of contemporary humanity. Suggested here is one of the prominent themes of later Russian literature: the spectral images of Petersburg evoked by Pushkin, Dostoevsky, and Andrey Bely, among others.

In "The Waterfall" (*Vodopad*), 1821, the preoccupation is with sound rather than time. At the center of its five stanzas, which are structured with reasoned clarity, stands the poet, lost in rapt meditation. The first of these, built on a sequence of imperatives, creates the picture of the waterfall, as the cascade of its grey torrent echoes in the valley. The second stanza resumes this description while simultaneously introducing the poetic personality; a fir tree is heard, rather than seen. Here and elsewhere euphony assists in thematic development: *slýshu—svíshchet; éliyu—nepogódoyu; revúshchey—ryóv* ("I hear"—"it whistles"; "fir tree"—"foul weather"; "howling"—"roar").

The center stanza, cast from two evenly-spaced questions, each beginning with the same word, concentrates on the poet alone and his almost mystical fascination with the waterfall:

> Why, with mad expectancy,
> Do I listen so to you?
> Why trembles thus my breast
> With some prophetic trembling? (79)

Behind the external features of the roaring water lies a suggestion
of concealed chaos, which finds a frantic response in the agitated
breast of the one bound to it in "mad expectancy."

Stanza four develops this motif, and, at the same time, constitutes
a move away from center, indicated by inclusion of physical details of nature:

> As if enchanted here I stand
> Above your hazy depths,
> And seemingly my heart perceives
> The wordlessness of your discourse. (79)

The correspondence between the void of formless delirium symbolized by the waterfall and the presence of an analogous, responsive element in the poet's consciousness finds more definite expression. "Discourse" (*rech*) is enveloped in an aura of mystery, embodied both in its archaic attributive (*bezglagolnaya*—"wordless")
and its resulting paradoxical status (oxymoron); "wordless discourse." This secret communion between the poet and nature,
which, in the following decade, became characteristic of a series
of Tyutchev's poems, was to account, in part, for the revival of Baratynsky's poetry by the Russian Symbolists over half a century later.

The last stanza, which completes the motion away from center,
is an exact repetition of the first:

> Resound, resound from lofty summit,
> Do not fall silent, leaden flow!
> Unite with your protracted wail
> Protracted answer of the valley. (79)

As such, it has the effect of intensifying the already concentrated
atmosphere: the poet and the waterfall are now locked in irrevocable unity, frozen, as it were, in unending spiritual communication.
This effect is accentuated by the rhyme scheme, in which identical
patterns link the first, third, and last stanzas.

The Classically-harmonious structure of "The Waterfall," reflected in the symmetrical disposition of its parts, is opposed to the

Romantically-chaotic core of its theme. This technique, manifested in the investing of irrational content with impeccably logical form, was to become a typical feature of Baratynsky's greatest verse.

The continuing penchant for opposites is expressed on another level in "Two Fates" (*Dve doli*), 1823, where the atmosphere of disillusionment bears a close relationship to many of the romantic elegies. The conflict of ideas set forth, rational experience versus spontaneity and hope, finds its source in Romanticism. But the blend of abstractness and reasoned consistency with which the conflict is worked out, together with the accompanying rhetorical tonality and the conclusion, both takes "Two Fates" beyond the usual limitations of elegiac canons and tends to counteract the emotional intensity felt beneath its exterior logic. As "To Delvig," it expands a peculiarly personal preoccupation into an all-embracing framework of universality.

The two basic sets of oppositions unfold in the first stanza: "hope and agitation" versus "hopelessness and peace." The contrast between these two possibilities, which are offered to the wisdom of an analytical mind, is underlined throughout by alternation of extended dactylic and concise masculine rhymes. Indicative of the precise rationalistic overtone is that in this stanza, as in each of the others, the line corresponds to a separate syntactic unit. Further, the rhythmic (---/---/--, ---/---/) and syntactic parallelism of the following two lines emphasizes in reverse the mutual antipathy of the opposites they contain: *Ili nadezhdu i volnenie,* / *Ili beznadezhnost i pokoy* ("Either hope and agitation, / Or hopelessness and peace") (91).

The category of "hope and agitation" is developed in the second and third stanzas and a constant outward projection is noted. Rhyming epithets, positioned evenly and placed under metrical stress, are formed from present active participles, which punctuate the active system of thought process that they embody, i.e., *obolshcháyushchiy* ("enticing"), *raznoveshcháyushchiy* ("speaking with many voices"), *kipyáshchie* ("seething"), *blestyáshchie* ("glittering").

Inexperience leads to hope: the passionate youths here are closely related to the "youthful jesters" described in Baratynsky's second epistle to Konshin, who are infatuated with the "blind thirst" for pleasure.

The second alternative is explored in the two succeeding stanzas, where euphonic devices and symmetrical balance in syntax are especially prominent. Past active participles, *ispytávshie* ("having

experienced"), *priyávshie* ("having accepted"), underscore the
finality of a reasoning which excludes the remotest possibility of
hope or enthusiasm. In such a vein were the sober reflections
of the "Imitation of LaFare," where, as here, a light "swarm" of
joys was contrasted with the cold thought of an "inactive soul."

The last two stanzas elaborate on the hopelessness of hope. Those
who continue to nurture desires are nurturing deceits, for they will
be rudely awakened from delusion by reality, as corpses roused
from insensibility by a sorceress, to face "new pain from former
wounds." The "seething youths" of stanza three have thus been
reduced to "reawakened corpses," to endure again the agonies
of existence, whereas their antitheses—those who recognize the
fallacies of "hope and agitation"—will continue to sleep on in
"blessed unconsciousness."

Herein lie both the negative attitude of such elegies as "The
Complaint," "Dissuasion" and "To Deliya," as well as components of the ideal of a quiet happiness. The suggestion of death
and the use of the concrete image of the corpses to symbolize an
abstract plane of thought anticipate the later Baratynsky.

"Truth" *(Istina)*, 1823, preserves essentially the logic of "Two
Fates," but lacks the systematic classification of opposites and
thereby strikes a more human note. It does resume, however,
the stylistic tonalities of the earlier poem, and the traditional
elegiac vocabulary assumes a new and broader significance.[10] The
beginning deals with the familiar theme of happiness, which continues to be elusive: the one who has longed for it since infancy
is still "poor in happiness."

The states of disillusionment in the mental biography are then
recapitulated, including the old incompatibility of desires with
life experience. The fourth stanza contains a deviation which would
have been impossible in the rigid framework of "Two Fates";
the painstaking analysis of a reflecting mind reveals that its process of disenchantment has not yet been completed. The soul can
still regret the loss of a notion of happiness connected with hope
and passion; in effect, it stands halfway between the categories of
"agitation" and "peace."

At this point "Truth" appears with her lamp and offers to show
the path to happiness; she prescribes about the same measures
of "hopelessness" and the concomitant "peace" which the poet
had prescribed for himself previously. What is striking is the

character of Truth itself, now embodied as a visible figure symbolizing an abstract concept. The intangible world of ideas merges with the material world of things in a specific psychological framework. Truth represents in concrete form—emphasized by the lamp of knowledge—a point of departure for an intellectual process; her appearance is the signal for the transformation from a personal, elegiac level to a generalized, metaphysical plane of reasoning.

Her lamp, however, illuminates the way to a torpid existence devoid of joy, and the poet, too weak to face its light, turns away in trepidation from his "fatal guest." He prefers, instead, to stumble along his own path, rejecting the logic he had so carefully built up. In the end he invites Truth to enlighten him, but only when he is on the edge of the grave, when he has passed the point of loving life. In such wise he wavers between two possibilities, chooses neither, and is left somewhere in between, dejected in his indecision.

These possibilities are expanded in "The Skull" *(Cherep)*, 1824, to embrace the ultimates of life and death. Baratynsky's concern with annihilation and death, noted in each of the two previous works, becomes a definite preoccupation, manifested in the form of a monologue addressed to a skull. Comprised of eight stanzas "The Skull" reveals a methodical development of theme and symmetrical balance in structure.

The first three stanzas, with their vivid, Naturalistic delineation, provide the backdrop; the disparity between the dead and the "thinking" organism of the living produces a keen emotional effect on the young man reflecting over the death's head:

> It still was wearing vestiges of hair;
> I saw on it the slow course of decay.
> A frightful sight! how violently impressed
> The thinking one—inheritor of ruin! (106)

It was this depiction that prompted Pushkin to speak of "Hamlet-Baratynsky" in an epistle to Delvig of 1827.[11]

In the next two stanzas concrete detail gives way to abstract meditation, in which the reckless comrades fade from sight and the image of the young man becomes a speculative category. This constitutes the highest point of tension as well as the heaviest concentration of archaic terminology. There is also a suggestion of the syntactic complexity typical of the poems of the *Twilight* collection. As elsewhere, the incongruity between life and death is a constant. Here it is embodied in a generalization portraying "flowering, passionate" youth threatened hourly by the stroke of death in lines given a singular unity by continued frequency of the case endings "im," "am," "om:"

> *Kogdá b ona tsvetúshchim, pýlkim nám*
> *I kázhdyy chás grozímym smértnym chásom*
> *Vse ístiny, izvéstnye grobám,*
> *Proizneslá svoim besstrástnym glásom!* (106)

> (What if it should, to flowering, passionate us
> And every hour menaced by death's hour
> All of the truths perceived by burial vaults,
> Communicate with its impassive voice!)

The "truths" from beyond the grave, however, will not be disclosed by the impartial voice of the skull. And the poet, realizing this, appears to be unreservedly relieved, just as he preferred not to learn "consoling impassivity" from the funereal lamp of "Truth." The bleak secret of the skull and his own cheerless conception of truth are uncomfortably similar in scope, and, hiding behind a rationalization, he praises the age-old law which respects the silence of the dead.

From this moment the intensity recedes and the final three stanzas are but variations on a theme of implied necessity. As mankind fails to ascend to the heights of his native sky ("To Delvig"), so does he fail in the other extreme—in his attempts to penetrate to the subterranean depths of the world of the dead. Suspended thus between heaven and the lower world and rebuffed in his quest for omniscience, he must make do with his halfway existence. Here he reaches an opposite conclusion than in "Two Fates" and simultaneously swings from the helpless frailty of his position in "Truth." In each of these he had tried to "smother natural feelings" (stanza eight, "The Skull"). Now he affirms their indispensability for the man living amidst the "noise of the world" but menaced by "the silence of the burial ground." The affirmation of life—even in the given conditions—is underlined by repetition of different forms of "to live" (*zhit*), and the shift to a more matter-of-fact atmosphere—quiet in its stoiclike inevitability—is stressed by the absence of Church Slavonicisms.

This untroubled, obvious solution proved to be but an expedient at best, and the calmness of "The Skull" disappears in the chaos of "The Storm" *(Burya)*, 1824. The latter is related to "The Waterfall" in that natural scenery, used as a point of departure, is transposed to a symbolic plane. It lacks the clear and consistent structure of the earlier poem; free iambic lines and a variety of individual rhyme patterns are woven together in a tangled patchwork. The raging of the elements is depicted in the opening lines, in which an exceptional number of verbs in active voice points up the motion of the storm.

Objective description subsequently receives broader significance and the external features of the storm take on a sinister ambiguity. The chaos of nature becomes representative of inner chaos, and the frenzy of the sea is transformed into the landscape of the mind. In it are focused the "desires, illness, passions and destruction"—the "grief"—that human nature is subjected to by dint of its instability. Silhouetted here are the thematic projections of a cycle of Baratynsky's poems, which crosses from "To Delvig" through "Two Fates," and "Truth" to "The Skull."

The principle of malice underlying the fury of the storm is a manifestation of the violent components of human temperament, and the power of its perpetrator, the "ruler of hell," is suggested in the picture of the earth trembling before the onslaught of "enormous wings" of roaring water. Artistic observation merges into the flow of deliberative meditation:

> When will the long-wished-for moment arrive?
> When will I place my faith, O ocean, in your waves?
> But know: the charm of distant lands
> Does not entice the flights of my imagination.
> Beneath a better heaven I
> Cannot meet with a better fate;
> I can't again allow my soul
> To flourish in a flowering land. (112, 113)

The symptoms of full disillusionment, accompanied by the impossibility of future gratification, point to a mental stagnation not unlike that of "Dissuasion" and "The Confession." But here impotency longs to dissolve itself in the movement of the storm, to become active for the sake of activity. As before, two potentials struggle for dominance in the personality, which itself becomes something of a schizophrenic in the process.

In this case the poet opts for the tumult implicit in the savagery of the sea: peace now becomes "cringing" to one who thirsts for self-deliverance at any price in the anarchy signified by the up-heavel at sea. Primeval chaos, with its attendant sway over reason, attracts a responsive element in human nature, an impulse for "long-desired struggle." This motif and that of restless yearning for agitation were to appear in the work of later Russian poets, among them, Lermontov, Tyutchev, and Blok.

Unable to abide either by the instructions of his reason or to listen to the sentiments of the heart, the poet falls into pandemonium. Nothing is resolved, nothing is settled in these poems: evidence of a dual attitude continues to be perceptible and finds expression in such diverse numbers as "Finland," "Rome," and "The Water-fall." The two "eternities" which he contains within himself in "Finland," for instance, can be expanded on other levels of meaning to embrace the contradictions of "Two Fates" as well as the ultimates he is obsessed with in "To Delvig" and "The Skull."

Further, in contrasting past and present in "Rome," it is as if he unconsciously attempted in his syntactic structure to compensate for the idea of the actual instability of Rome; as if he romantically searched for a symbol of eternity, failed to find it, then softened the edge of his disillusionment by devising a solid and reasoned verse structure in which a great city becomes a ghost. Elegiacal and, at the same time, sincere disillusionment and a determination not to give in to it—herein are the hallmarks of these works.

IV   The Epistles

The friendly epistle, which was a favorite genre among the poets in Petersburg, was, as the elegy, another legacy of French Classicism. The epistles of such poets as Pushkin, Delvig, Baratyn-sky, and Vyazemsky appeared often on the pages of literary publications of the time; they tended to be congenial, even intimate, and were written, for the most part, in iambic.

The otherwise hackneyed "To Krenitsyn" (*K Krenitsynu*), 1819, demonstrates Baratynsky's inclination to convert the conventional friendly epistle into a means for serious deliberation. It also is worthy of note that it is his first poetic expression both of a rationalistic bent and of a tendency to posit irreconcilable opposites. In this epistle, with its elegiac theme of a lost happiness and untimely disillusionment, the poet wonders what has become of "former dreams" and "the joy of hope" and provides his own reply with an air of finality: "Chill experience has destroyed all" (46). Identified with experience is "reason," which is in direct conflict with "happiness."

The "Epistle to B[aron] Delvig" *(Poslanie k B[aronu] Delvigu)*, 1820, containing elements of autobiography and traditional epicureanism, ends on a note of despondency. Past happiness is juxtaposed with the more melancholy present, set against the waters and rocks of Finland. Various motifs are blended together by use of alliterative lines and recurrent terminology, the latter involving roughly half of all the three hundred words in the poem. This device sharply pinpoints opposite implications and creates chains of images given a striking effect by dint of the resulting mutual associations. For example, sparkling wine *(blestyashchee vino)* is delicately linked with the brilliance *(blesk)* of summer lightning, which lends the wine an added glow and stresses the transience of its "oblivion."

In Baratynsky's first epistle to Konshin, "To K—n" *(K—nu)*, 1820, deterministic moods of distress are relieved only by a perception of possible harmony and peace in a "sensitive friend." In the aphoristic ending use of recurrent terminology receives an unexpected turn in the juxtaposition of *chuvstvennost* ("sensuality") and *chuvstvo* ("feeling"). Sound similarities are preserved, but in context each word is lexically opposed to the other, and in this opposition is capsuled the thought process of the epistle. This precision and compression of expression distinguishes Baratynsky's poetry from that of his contemporaries and also illustrates how he developed to its ultimate complexity one of the basic devices of Batyushkov.

In the second epistle, 1821, to his friend, passion and desire have retreated: "irrational amusements" are relegated to the past. The poet, in attempting to forestall the "inevitable offenses" of the future, rejects the frenzies of the past; a "more experienced heart" must seek happiness, not sensual ecstasies. Here, too, an escape from the dilemma of these polemics is pointed out in the need for a quiet type of happiness and a "tender friend." The last missive to

Konshin, "Good Advice" *(Dobryy sovet)*, 1821, is opposed to the first two in that brooding tones of sadness are transformed into light epicureanism.

"To..." *(K ...)*, 1821, is addressed to the journalist-writer Faddey Bulgarin. Continuing indications of disillusionment are specified more definitely:

> In a soul made ill by many trials,
> In a wearied soul the flame has died,
> And over a cheerful glass of drink
> Stern experience chanced to find us. (75)

The same process of collision of youth with the more sober realities of maturity is noted, but that process is associated with "stern experience," as in the epistle to Krenitsyn. The conventional concrete tropes of the poetry of youth and revelry are retained, but are employed in a framework wherein they denote a psychological condition—a technique characteristic of Baratynsky's later verse.

The reaction of early disenchantment with life consisted of a certain blend of reconciliation and renunciation. In "To Comrades" *(Tovarishcham)*, 1821, the poet confesses in meek, somber tones that the years have indeed changed him, that he has replaced "turbulent happiness" with "quiet gratification." He tries to find a rational clarification of the inner development which has caused him to close his door to "merry-makers"; this "retired jester" reasons thus:

> In the first flame of youthful days
> Our passions are invincible:
> We frolic under their command
> While having lost control of self. (83)

In many of these epistles there are elements of the then-fashionable theme of severing ties of friendship because of incapacity to lead the former careless existence of carousing and merrymaking; but there are also indications of genuine disillusionment and of a perplexed attempt to adjust to new conditions occasioned by age and maturity.

Unlike the previous epistles, Baratynsky's two missives to Gnedich (1823) follow the stylistic traditions of French Classicism. In the first of these, "To N. I. Gnedich" *(N. I. Gnedichu)*, the author seeks to emulate his friend as poet and scholar. Autobiographical passages are interspersed with didactic pronouncements on idleness and art; the undistinguished alexandrine couplets are overburdened with numerous repetitions of semantic doublets.

More interesting is the second epistle "To Gnedich, Who Advised the Author to Write Satires" (*Gnedichu, kotoryy sovetoval sochinitelyu pisat satiry*), written as a response to Gnedich's call for a poetry impregnated with civic and social ideals.[12] This epistle constitutes one of the few exceptions to Baratynsky's general silence in regard to literary debates. Unlike Pushkin, Vyazemsky, and others of his poet-friends, he usually refrained from engaging in polemics in the press.

In this verse reply to Gnedich he refuses to turn the "light sounds" of his "shepherd's reed pipe" into the "restless barking" of satire. While agreeing that the impartial satirist is useful to society, he justifies his reluctance to participate on the grounds of his "peace-loving disposition" and unworthiness, plus the general ineffectiveness of satire and the lack of appreciation afforded its writer by a public engrossed in its own mediocrity. The didacticism and rationalist manner of the epistle are placed in the service of the status quo—deterministically represented by the inability of the aspen tree to become an oak and vice versa.

The didactic tone and alexandrines of these epistles are resumed in "To Bogdanovich" (*Bogdanovichu*), 1824. Addressed to the eighteenth-century poet, "To Bogdanovich" is directly related to the preceding epistle in that the author uses it as a vehicle for expression of literary opinions, which, in themselves, were indicative of his own position in the middle of the 1820's.

It was written at a time of sharp controversy and polemical initiative, which embraced such widely divergent phenomena as Katenin's fight for acceptance of colloquial language in serious poetry and the Decembrist poets' demand for aggressive personalities and positive ideas, as well as more general and comprehensive discussions concerned with rhyme, meter, and genre. Kyukhelbeker's article "On the Trends of Our Poetry, Especially Lyrical, in the Last Decade" (*O napravlenii nashey poezii, osobenno liricheskoy, v poslednee desyatiletie*), which called for originality in Russian verse, was suggestive of the atmosphere. Reacting against elegiac poetry, he wrote: "Read any elegy of Zhukovsky, Pushkin or Baratynsky, you know everything."[13] Baratynsky's epistle undoubtedly has connections with this article.[14]

"To Bogdanovich" is a kind of assessment of the contemporary

"Russian Parnassus." The "newest poets," of whom Zhukovsky was
the first, are those captivated by "the spleen of German muses";
these are taken up with withered souls and faded hearts. This
description recalls, to a certain extent, the nature of much of
Baratynsky's own early elegiac poetry. However, Kyukhelbeker
had brought to task not only the followers of German trends but
also those of French Classical traditions. Baratynsky omits any
reference to the latter, which, like the style and genre of his epistle,
probably implied where his loyalties lay. Accordingly, in opposing
another standard to that of current literary practices, he turns to
eighteenth-century Classicism.

In a shift to the present he launches a caustic and satirical attack
on literary journalists and their "commercial logic." Batyushkov,
Zhukovsky, and Pushkin are singled out as genuine talents, and
writing of himself, the poet surveys the characteristic features of
his personal talent. The didacticism of this passage notwithstanding, it enumerates several of the fundamental distinctions of
Baratynsky's work, including his concern with form and his preoccupation with "intellect" and "thought."

Apart from this preoccupation, his inclinations toward analy-
tic techniques, as well as the rationalistic stamp of his poetic
thought, were accepted by his contemporaries as holdovers from the
Classicism of the past century. For example, in regard to the above
epistle, Delvig wrote to Pushkin of its "unfortunate didacticism."[15]

The internal dialectic between passion and reason is taken up in
"To D—g" (D—gu), 1825, addressed to Delvig, and is dealt with
in a typically reflective manner; it dissolves in an epicurean conclusion. The dialectic reappears, however, in "To L.S. P—n" (L.S.
P—nu), 1825, addressed to Pushkin's younger brother:

> But me, let me conceal the unavailing flame,
> At times engendered by a fleeting glimpse of beauty,
> Dispute the fancies of the heart with intellect
> And with a chilly smile withhold from sight my feeling. (121)

The continually recurring dichotomy between the "heart" and
the "intellect," reflected in so much of Baratynsky's poetic work,
is once again stated here in frank and simple terms. It is implicit
in most of these epistles, and corresponds to the opposition between
"happiness" and "reason" noted in the poem addressed to Krenitsyn, as well as to the collision between past and present, youth

and "experience," expressed in that and succeeding epistles. The poet repeatedly vacillates between one and the other or seeks refuge in an epicurean escape, behind which his pessimistic confusion is painfully apparent. The motif of the "tender friend"—a vision of harmony and inner peace—remains undeveloped.

V *The Medley*

Baratynsky's early versatility is perhaps best manifested in this group of poems, which fall broadly within several genre classifications of Classical French *poésie légère*, ranging from occasional verse to the traditional despondent elegy.

Belonging to the latter category is "Dejection" *(Unynie)*, 1821, which unfolds in an undoubtedly autobiographical setting of "regimental brothers" and revelry. The poet, having drowned his "intellect" in wine—recalling the oblivion afforded by the full cup in the "Epistle to B[aron] Delvig"—is nevertheless prevented by the relentless trend of thought from joining this revelry. Instead he remains apart, locked within himself and his anguish; deterministic "fate" permits no outlet to untimely gloom.

On the contrary, in "Home" *(Rodina)*, 1821, he finds an escape in conventional praising of quiet country happiness. In a technical sense this elegy of sixty lines written in alexandrine couplets is remarkable for its lack of verbal rhyme.[16]

During 1821, which was one of Baratynsky's most prolific years, his poetry dealt with a diversity of themes. "To Lida" *(Lide)*, an Anacreontic poem filled with Classical imagery, is concerned with the essential integrity and solitude of the poet; implied here also is the Romantic idea of the incommunicability of the poetic process.

Finnish nature merges with lyrical reflection in "Departure" *(Otezd)*, 1821. The "lifeless spring," "eternal rustling of the pines," "roar of the sea," "moss-grown heaps of stones," "naked fields," and "age-old waterfalls"—all this nourished the "madness of gloomy thoughts" and furnished a landscape which lent animation and color to the trends of poetic contemplation. In effect, it became symbolic of a frame of mind, for which its grey outlines and somber features provided an appropriate visual setting. This natural scenery of Finland gave a special tonality to much of Baratynsky's verse during these years, as did that of the Russian South to Pushkin's poetry during the same period.

"Spring" (Vesna), 1822, a hymn to spring, is appealing in its euphony and descriptive detail. The lively movement of the first four stanzas becomes a pensive meditation in the last four. On the other hand, "The Falling of Leaves" (Padenie listev), 1823, a translation from Charles Hubert Millevoye's "La chute des feuilles," presents a traditional parallel of autumn and the death of a youth.

"Hopelessness" (Beznadezhnost), 1823, is by its very title, connected with "Two Fates." The beginning, however, recalls specifically "To Delvig," where the dilemma of being suspended between heaven and earth is again given expression. The conclusion continues the ideas of "Two Fates," and in similar tones of resignation, the poet arrives at a corresponding decision and renounces a living happiness to obtain a detached tranquility, which "resembles happiness." The immobility of his position is fixed by the contrast between his "rest" and the movement of the "passers-by."

"To..." (K...), 1824-1825, addressed to the general's wife, Zakrevskaya, is a psychological miniature in superbly finished form. With skill and finesse the characterization of a woman who weeps like a Magdalene and laughs like a water nymph is traced by the observant poet.[17] Opposite in this respect is the impression produced by Aleksandra Voeykova, the subject of "To A. A. V—a" (A. A. V—oy), 1826, whose ethereal beauty entices from "earthly life" and fills the soul with a "sacred calm."

As before, the principles of eighteenth-century Classicism continued to be manifest in Baratynsky's poetry, as—to a somewhat lesser extent—did those of Romanticism. Indicative of a Romanticist leaning was his inclination to disregard the Classical system of genres, in evidence in his work as early as 1820. Such an inclination was characteristic of other poets of the time, in particular, of Pushkin.

"Stanzas" (Stansy), 1825, shows a breakdown of the rules of Classical procedure in this sense. At the same time it contains unmistakable traces of didacticism and reveals a logical move from the general to the particular. Its determinism is reminiscent of earlier poems, but it offers a possibility of escape from despondency. Despite the detachment of "indifference," the glimmer of a positive attitude is perceptible in the turn to poetry for consolation: the gods are "justified" and the poet is given new strength to see him through his quandary. Poetry thus assumes a more definite function here than in the art-for-art motifs of "Finland" and the epistle to Bogdanovich.

Dejection, however, pervades "The Road of Life" (*Doroga zhizni*), 1825, an eight-line miniature built on the development of a single metaphor which becomes an allegory;[18] the unfolding metaphor is constantly supported by appropriate terminology. A typically analytical division into two equal parts depicts the confident youth in the first, who, as a sober, mature individual in the second, pays with his dreams for the disillusionment of life. This division is upheld by an equal break in the rhyme: the rhyming vowel in the first stanza, "a," becomes "y" in stanza two.

Use of the prosaic expression *izvestnyy zapas* ("a certain stock"), which contrasts with the Church Slavonic *blagaya* ("benignant"), throws the fantasies of youthful dreams into greater focus and prepares the way for the irony of the two concluding lines:

> Benignant fate presents to us
> A certain stock of golden dreams.
> . . . .
> And with those fatal dreams we pay
> The traveling costs of life. (119)

"The Inscription" (*Nadpis*), 1826, another of the Classical genres, recalls the structure of "Reassurance" in its even partitioning of statement and figurative treatment of statement. The depiction of a cold, indifferent face merges into that of a congealed waterfall, suspended motionlessly over an abyss. This waterfall, "preserving the semblance of motion" (123), bears a close affinity to the frozen streams near the end of "Eda," which hang in icy masses against a backdrop of granite mountains. And as passion is chilled into unyielding rigidity there, so is it here: the "trace" of past emotion remains in perpetually fixed insensibility.

Agitation is thus turned into inertia, hope is converted into resignation, and sentiment becomes impassivity—these distinctive features of an entire trend in Baratynsky's early poetry are symbolized in the immobility of a frozen waterfall. The poet essays to destroy within himself the wells of feeling, to suppress individual passion with a formal intellectualism. This aspiration, Classical in its implications, which is embodied in partiality for the static and repression of the personal, could not fail to be reflected in over-all selection of imagery and in lyrical structure; the one tends to suggest the abstract, whereas the other is often subordinated to a consistent logic.

o   o   o   o

In 1827 Baratynsky's first book of poems was published. This collection, structured on a somewhat traditional basis, was divided into five major sections: three "books" of elegies, a "medley" (*smes*) of various genres, and the epistles. However, this system proved to be artificial and purely external to a large extent.[19] In this connection the collection as a whole was illustrative of that move away from the limitations of the Classical genre system, which, as mentioned before, was typical of a general trend in Russian poetry during the 1820's.

Many of the eighty-three lyrics, as well as the longer "Telema and Makar" that were printed there had been substantially revised several times. In general, Baratynsky subjected his work to constant revision, as is evident both from the numerous variants of his poems published in the periodicals of the time and the existing draft copies. It is characteristic that the principles he was guided by in incorporating these changes should reflect the inner struggle that found expression in so much of his poetry on one level or another.

In one of his two critical articles, "A. Muravyov's 'Tavrida'" ("*Tavrida*" A. *Muravyova*), 1827, which dealt with the minor poet, Andrey Muravyov, Baratynsky wrote:

True poets are rare just because they must simultaneously possess qualities which completely contradict one another: the blaze of creative imagination and the cold of restraining intellect. As far as style is concerned, one must remember that we write in order to communicate our thoughts to one another; if we express ourselves inexactly, we are falsely understood or understood not at all: why write, then?[20]

A year later he was even more precise in a letter to Putyata: "The pride of the intellect and the rights of the heart are in continual struggle. You like a certain poem owing to recollection of the feeling with which it is written. You take pride in the revision because you have overcome with intellect the feeling of the heart."[21]

The implications of this attitude are apparent. In his painstaking corrections Baratynsky gradually lessened or eliminated entirely the autobiographical elements in his verse, together with the more obvious of the conventional and elegiac features inherited from Batyushkov. On this basis he even excluded certain elegies from the collection, as well as epigrams which carried personal allusions. As a result of his reworkings, many of his poems were shortened. His poetic language became more exact, his style more compressed. Too, his verse tended to acquire a more formal and studied atmosphere at the expense of spontaneity.[22]

The collection was received by the critics and the public with moderate enthusiasm, for the most part. In Baratynsky's own poetic evolution it is representative of a crucial point: it contains most of the important work of his first years of creativity and pinpoints significant stages in the continual unfolding of that work.

It shows him as an early imitator of the traditional elegy and traces his subsequent transformation of the elegy from a vehicle for the expression of conventional feelings into an instrument both for recording the most intricate and delicate shades of psychological feeling and for presenting, in weighted and abstract tones, the manifold contradictions of existence. It demonstrates how he developed to its ultimate extent, in these respects, the possibilities of the elegy as a genre, and then proceeded to move beyond it. At the same time the collection reveals the beginnings of a new period in Baratynsky's artistic evolution, the consequences of which were to be reflected in his poetic outlook as a whole.

CHAPTER 3

The Long Poems

B ARATYNSKY'S desire to write more ambitious works was apparent as early as 1820 and is reflected in a series of seven poems, written during the first half of his creative period. Despite his persistent interests in this direction, these poems, with few exceptions, are characterized by over-all ineffectiveness and short-comings.

I *The Shorter Works*

"Fragments from the Poem 'Reminiscences'" (*Otryvki iz poemy 'Vospominania'*), 1820, a free translation of Gabriel Marie Legouvais' (1764-1812) "Les souvenirs, ou les avantages de la mémoire," represents Baratynsky's first attempt at a long poem. It is, as the title suggests, a hymn to memory. Constructed on Classical principles and written in bland alexandrine couplets, it is didactic, diffuse, and lacks any hint of motion. Perhaps its major significance lies in several of its motifs, that is, traditional praising of the quiet happiness and solitude of the country as opposed to the "vain glitter" of worldly life and conventional fascination with ancient ruins; these were to find better expression in shorter poems.

Baratynsky's most successful work in this line, which won for him, in the words of Pushkin, the reputation of "the poet of feasts and languid melancholy,"[1] was "Feasts" (*Piry*), 1820. "Feasts" was an early reflection (Pushkin's "Ruslan and Lyudmila" was another) of that breakup and final disintegration of the rigid system of Classical genres, which was connected with the introduction of Romantic trends. As it contains elements of more than one genre, it falls out of the system of Classical poetics. To a certain extent a parallel development may be seen in Derzhavin's poetry, when he combined, for instance, elements of the ode and the satire in "Felitsa."

"Feasts," whose 200 lines are written in the ever-popular iambic tetrameter, is divided into eight unequal parts. Its various themes—eating, friendship and the collision between youth and maturity—were widespread both in Russian poetry and in French *poésie légère*,[2] and had found earlier expression in Baratynsky's own verse. Written near the end of his first year in Finland when he was twenty, the poem carries an undoubtedly autobiographical tonality.

It begins in a light, uncharacteristically ironic tone, embodied in the humorous rhyming of "intellect" (*rassúdok*) and "stomach" (*zhelúdok*). The invocation to friends (to Pushkin and Delvig, in particular) is constant throughout and forms a leitmotif which succeeds in binding the different parts and moods together. In spite of the irony of the introductory lines, the attitude is one of a reflective individual, pausing to survey the past: "My soul was full of fuss and bustle, / And long I followed beaten trails. . . ." (221).

But carefree flippancy dominates the first half, and the third part, which initiates a move from the general to the particular, constitutes a good-natured satirical depiction of aristocratic Moscow society and its devotion to banquets. In his efforts, however, to do justice to the lavish impression of "dainty dishes" and "heaps of golden fruits" and the desserts shining through a "clear, light steam," the poet selects the following comparison:

> But thus rows of ancient graves
> Beneath the spring's awakening skies
> Shine forth with purple rays of light
> Under the haze of morning mists. (223)

An image of ancient burial mounds appears in the midst of splendor and youth; an image of death sits on the table surrounded by the frolicsome guests, who eagerly await the meal—the climax of irony. Reminiscent of Derzhavin, this subtle portrayal functions as a forewarning and assists in preparing the transition to the dejected mood of the second half of the poem.

Elements of disenchantment and gloom characterize this half, distinctly elegiac in tone. The days of love have passed away and high-spirited comrades have been separated by "stern fate":

> And each, murmuring, heaved a sigh,
> And extended a hand to his friend,
> And set out on his own far path;
> And each in mute despondency
> Perhaps in idle flight of fancy
> Recalls by now the bygone days. . . . (225)

The feasts of youth become a memory and the poet, older now,
sits at another, quieter table. These notes of solitude were to find
their highest expression in *Twilight* some twenty years later.
Another suggestion of isolation is apparent in the picture of the
anchorite, which opens the last part of "Feasts." Maturity and
experience are implicit in the following passage:

> From the day of parting, this I know,
> That days and years have flown away,
> And we've been able to resolve
> Much that lay concealed in life;
> No matter what seduced us then,
> No matter what possessed the heart—
> As though it were a morning dream,
> All has betrayed, has passed away! (226)

Although the same man as in the first part of the poem—with
his tendency to reflect—is in evidence here, the atmosphere and
tonality have significantly changed. Gone are the laughing irony
and the flippancy. The one who jokingly asserted in the beginning
that "not all in the world has betrayed me" (221), now admits
that "all has betrayed, has passed away" like a "morning dream,"
a simile which evokes the lines of ancient graves under the cover
of "morning mists."

Accordingly, "Feasts" closes in a minor key, as do many of Baratynsky's shorter poems, in which light tones are not sustained and
tend to disintegrate into melancholy. Much of the charm and appeal
of "Feasts" springs from the author's lyricism, which harmonizes
various themes and sentiments. Its internal lyrical development
is individual and complex, yet transitions are made smoothly
through the use of parallel syntactic constructions, recurrence of
key words and images, and that reflecting element of the poetic
personality which imposes balance and restraint on lyrical effusion.

A happy past is opposed to a pensive present; feelings inspired
by gladness and good humor correspond to the period of youth,
those inspired by dejection are connected with maturity. In a
general context "Feasts" can be read as an expression of loss of
youthful enthusiasm and ideals. In more restricted terms, much
of its coloring and atmosphere, as well as certain of its details,
stem from Baratynsky's "exile" with the Russian army in Finland.

Written in another vein are Baratynsky's two didactic tales,
which, in contrast to "Feasts," demonstrate his continuing loyalty
to both the ideas and conventions of French Classicism. The first

of these, "Telema and Makar" (*Telema i Makar*), 1827, is a translation of Voltaire's "Thélème et Macare." Composed of 126 lines in iambic tetrameter, it is a short narrative of "Desire" and "Happiness." Even though Baratynsky did not include the moralistic conclusion of the original and made some effort to transfer the setting to Russia, the poem remains fundamentally French in technique and spirit. Its outcome, which preaches an undemanding happiness in preference to the restlessness of desire, ties it directly to a similar line in his lyric verse.

The longer "The Transmigration of Souls" (*Pereselenie dush*), 1828-1829, is reminiscent of the previous poem in its conventionality. Here the discord is between love and duty, but on a fantastic, fairy-tale level. Stylized setting and atmosphere are augmented by mock solemnity, resplendent imagery and lines of extraordinary euphony, i.e., *Chelóm belée líliy Níla* (266). In accord with its appealing stylization is the light and graceful movement of the iambic tetrameter; for example:

> *Blistáyut rédkimi tsvetámi*
> *Ryadý uzórchatykh koshníts,*
> *I pólon vózdukh golosámi*
> *Dalnozemélnykh, chúdnykh ptíts;*
> *Vsyo négoy sládostnoyu dýshit,*
> *Vsyo dívnoy róskoshiyu pýshet.* (270)

In this passage, as well, is one of the two instances of unstressed "i"-"e" rhyme (*dyshit—pyshet*) found in the poem, a rhyme which was not to become popular in Russian poetry until the next decade.

The conclusion, forming an epilogue, is addressed to Baratynsky's wife and carries other personal nuances, noted especially in the search in poetry for a release from inner difficulties. The "friend" recalls the epistles to Konshin:

> At times I reconciled with verse
> The impulse of afflicting passions;
> Although the sorrow of the soul
> To me was painful inspiration.
> Then you appeared, my cherished friend,
> And life became suffused with light. (273)

Unlike his more lengthy narrative poems, in which Baratynsky could not harmoniously integrate a variety of trends and moods, here he successfully combines levity with didacticism, lyricism with strict adherence to Classically prescribed form.

II *Eda*

During the autumn of 1824 Baratynsky began to write an extended and consciously Romantic work—"Eda." It is doubtlessly true that he plunged himself into this work at the behest of his literary friends, who were disappointed by his persistent attachment to the language and stylistic traditions of Classicism; it may also be true that there was some desire on his own part to abandon the strictly elegiac side of his early poetry.

The examples of the long poems of both Byron and Pushkin were already before Baratynsky. In the interest of originality he wished to avoid their influence, as is made clear by the preface to the 1826 edition of "Eda," in which he states: "He [the author] did not assume a lyrical tone in his tale, not being so bold as to enter into competition with the bard of 'The Captive of the Caucasus' and 'The Fountain of Bakhchisaray.'...To follow Pushkin seemed to him more difficult and courageous than to take a new and independent path" (383).

The components of this "independent path" were suggested in the same preface: "...the author could be mistaken, but it seemed to him that in poetry two opposite paths lead almost to the same end: the very unusual and the absolutely simple, alike impressing the intellect and alike engaging the imagination" (383). It was the "absolutely simple" that Baratynsky attempted to portray in "Eda" as opposed to the "very unusual" of Pushkin's Southern poems.

The plot of "Eda" is not unlike that of "The Captive of the Caucasus" (*Kavkazskiy plennik*) in its conventionality: the love of a simple, uneducated girl for a civilized individual, a theme which found its ultimate source in Rousseau. As in Pushkin's poems there is an historical setting, in this case, the prosaic wilds of southeastern Finland in the period immediately preceding the Russo-Swedish War of 1808-1809, in contrast to the heady, exotic scenery of the Caucasus during the years of its struggle for independence. The characters of "Eda," though bearing an external resemblance to those of "The Captive," are basically different.[3] Eda, for example, assumes the leading role in a story named for her; her image is at once Romantic and highly idealized: both her face and her soul are radiant with beauty.

The character of the hussar, however, remains ambiguous and ill-defined. His pose of Byronic disillusionment and the aura of melodrama surrounding him, together with details of appearance and biography of earlier redactions, were discarded by Baratynsky in the version prepared for the 1835 collection of his works. In the final analysis, he is both sensitive and callous in his relationship with Eda.

If the hussar represents a step in the direction of Realism, then the two secondary characters, Eda's parents, are a step further in that direction. The suspicious father, depicted pacing back and forth in his room and banging his fist on a table as he lectures a trembling Eda, is especially well-drawn. His language, coarse and direct in its vividness, reflects his peasant background and his clipped, aphoristic manner is often accentuated by enjambments. This incisive psychological portrait is but an example of the over-all psychological treatment of the other characters in connection with the movement of the plot.

The Romantically-inspired and, at the same time, Realistically exact digressions on Finnish nature are psychologized, as well, and are inseparably woven into Eda's destiny.[4] From the beginning her features tend to merge with those of the landscape: her pale-blue eyes reflect the Finnish sky. The description of her as "a rose of the first spring days," caressed by a warm breeze further points up the correspondence. Spring in nature is her spring in love—this hackneyed parallel is saved from banality by a projection of the psychological method: "For you the captivating spring/With its enchanting bliss is dreadful" (231).

Moreover, in one of several bursts of lyricism denied by the preface, the author continues:

> Don't listen to the sweet-voiced bird!
> From sleep arisen, from the porch
> Your face toward the morning cool
> Don't turn, and in the lovely dale
> Do not appear, but this above all—
> Seclude yourself from your hussar! (231)

Eda's placid happiness is first disturbed when the hussar, who is billeted in her household, succeeds in kissing her. Night overtakes the two of them as they sit together and her confusion is accordingly set forth in terms of natural phenomena: morning is invested with the dusk of evening. From this moment her transformation from a carefree, innocent girl into an impassioned mistress begins. This transformation is traced by the author step by step with striking fidelity to the actuality of psychological experience. As in his lyrics, Baratynsky's skillful use of recurrent terminology adds to the depth of the over-all effect. Eda, for instance, becomes more and more helpless in her relationship with the hussar: "But then she sometimes from his eyes / Her pensive eyes does not remove . . ." (233).

She is unable to tear her eyes away from his; however, another set of eyes is watching her with equal, but different, intensity—that of her father: "He his suspicious gaze did not/From the unhappy maid remove; . ." (233). This impressionistic interplay of eyes serves to pinpoint her inner state of contradiction and her incipient tragedy; she is caught between the eyes of the hussar and her father, or, on another level, between love and duty.

Recurrent terminology is also used to produce ironic effects. In an early conversation Eda reveals her fears to her future lover:

> " . . . They say,
> . . . .
> That you somehow destroy us,
> . . . .
> Perhaps you will destroy me."—
> " I, your destroyer, Eda, I?" (229, 230)

Later, in the heat of seduction, he hypocritically tells her:

> " I gave free rein to hapless love
> And I destroyed, trusting it,
> . . . .
> All the bliss of my future days." (235)

Similar results occur in the use of such words as "duty" *(dolg)* and "trust" *(doveryatsya)*.

The night of their first assignation is again accompanied by a meaningful parallel in nature, given an emphatic overtone by the unusual use of the noun *mrak* ("darkness") in the plural: "Already both the hills and fields / Are covered with thick darknesses" (237).

Attention is also focused on the door to Eda's room by accumulated repetition, and in this connection, the door becomes the turning point in the narrative. When she unlocks it to the hussar she enters into a new existence, far removed from her past innocence and virtue. At this crucial point her indecisiveness is indicated by the back and forth motion of her hands; the motion of "another hand," however, in opening the door she has at last unlocked, renders her decision irrevocable. Eda goes beyond the point of no return, and the change in her situation and internal state is duly commented on by the author.

The summer passes. Eda becomes increasingly agitated over the thought that she will be abandoned, whereas the hussar vacillates between remorse and tedium. The dilemma is solved for both of them by history; he is called away by the outbreak of war between Russia and Sweden in 1808. Eda realizes that he will not return, and the change in her is now complete: her face and soul, no longer sparkling with radiant beauty, have become "lifeless." Winter arrives. The flowing streams harden into ice and the blue skies disappear in a cold, grey mist. The dead and spectral face of winter replaces the brightly-hued flowers of spring. Eda has undergone a similar transformation; as pale as the winter sky, she sits motionlessly at her window.

The passions of summer are now frozen into immobility, and only the violent snow storms remind of their once-vibrant existence. However, the storms awaken no response in Eda, who sees in them only her shroud. Her warm spring breeze has developed into raging winds; in the same way her passion had become unrestrained and led, in the end, to her destruction. The transition to death is easy, and the narrative closes with a sentimental description of her grave, disturbed only by the whistling of the wind and the rustling of the juniper. The poem concludes with an epilogue (published first in 1860) praising the Finns for their courage and resistance during the war.

The final version of "Eda" consists of 652 lines, all in iambic tetrameter. As in Pushkin's Southern poems, there is neither a division into stanzas of equal length nor a consistent rhyming pattern. More so than in his lyrics of the time, Baratynsky makes use of Church Slavonicisms in "Eda," thereby heightening its stylized atmosphere; adding yet more to the stylization effect is the euphony of lines such as Drevésnoy vétkoy otveváet (239) and S litsá zemlí moy lyógkiy sléd (242).

Despite the technical proficiency embodied in its polished iambs, its expert application of devices, including enjambment and recurrent terminology, and its sensitive and detailed psychological portrayal, Baratynsky did not create a "new, independent path." Because of external similarity in story, characters, and epilogue, "Eda" was inevitably compared with Pushkin's long poems, especially "The Captive of the Caucasus." Moreover, the lyricism disclaimed by the preface represented a direct carry-over fom the Romanticism of both Pushkin and Byron.[5] Critics were quick to note that the figure of Eda, in its sentimentality—she gives way to tears seven times—and idealization recalled Karamzin's "Poor

Liza"; Belinsky scornfully dismissed "Eda" as a "'Poor Liza' in verse."[6]

Baratynsky's aspiration toward the "absolutely simple" was reflected in the convincing psychological overtones of Eda's experience, the descriptions of Northern landscape, inclusion of petty details touching Finnish peasant life, and elements of simple and colloquial speech. Pushkin appreciated these factors of Realism and in a letter to Delvig, he exclaimed: "...—What a charm this Eda is! Our critics will not understand the originality of the story. But what variety! The hussar, Eda, and the poet himself, each speaks in his own way. And the description of Livonian [sic] nature! and the morning after the first night! and the scene with the father!—a marvel!"[7]

And in 1828, when working on his projected article, "Baratynsky's 'The Ball'" ("Bal"Baratynskogo) he wrote of "Eda": "...a work so remarkable in its original simplicity, charm of story, liveliness of colors and sketch of characters, slightly, but skillfully delineated,...."[8] Finally, two years later, Pushkin again turned to "Eda" in his unfinished article, "Baratynsky": "Reread this simple, delightful tale; you will see with what depth of feeling feminine love is developed in it."[9]

The publication of "Eda" was coincidental with the beginnings of Realistic tendencies in Russian literature. But Baratynsky did not succeed in really integrating these tendencies into his compositional method. Consequently, the poem presents a somewhat fragmented and contradictory appearance. For example, the psychological veracity clashes with Eda's stylized image and the details of peasant life conflict with the lyricism. Moreover, Eda and the hussar hardly satisfied the demands of the time for fiery and exotic personalities.

Baratynsky himself perceived the deficiencies of his work and in his preface he had asserted: "The author feels the shortcoming of his verse experiment" (383). The tone of all the preface approaches apology and doubt; he was unsure of himself both in the sphere of the unfamiliar genre of the long poem and in its intended Romanticist character. "Eda" was an expression, in brief, of an attempt to broaden himself, to demonstrate his versatility in areas other than the fundamentally reflective type of lyric verse that preceded it. A product of a deliberate and calculated effort to be different, it fell somewhat short of the mark.

Ashamed of his inadequacy, he confessed in a letter (in French) to Kozlov in January, 1825:

I blush to speak of Eda. . . . I think that a bit too much of vanity led me astray: I did not want to follow the beaten track, I did not want to imitate either Byron or Pushkin; that's why I threw myself into prosaic details, endeavoring to put them in verse; thus, all I got was rhymed prose. Wanting to be original, I have been only odd.[10]

"Eda" met with a mixed reaction in the literary press. Despite Pushkin's delight, others of Baratynsky's poet-friends were disappointed. Yazykov write of "Eda" in 1826: "too little of poetry, too much of the unseemly, the commonplace and, consequently, the old; there are a few good depictions and that's all."[11] And Bestuzhev complained in a letter to Pushkin: "His 'Edda' [*sic*] is a mark of insignificance, both in subject matter and in execution. . . ."[12] "Eda" proved to be Baratynsky's "first creative tragedy"[13] and signified the beginning of the disintegration of his popularity.

III *The Ball*

Even before the basic revision of "Eda" was completed, Baratynsky had begun another long poem, "The Ball" *(Bal)*, first published in full in 1828 under the same cover as Pushkin's "Count Nulin" *(Graf Nulin)*. This time he did not seek to avoid the influence of either Pushkin or Byron: his two main characters are openly Byronic.

The Princess Nina, modeled on Zakrevskaya, is endowed with a complex and impassioned nature; her chaste lips mock feminine virtue and society is weary of talk concerning her "shameless conquests." Her contradictory qualities are drawn sharply by recurrence of identical words in contexts where they have opposite implications:

> How captivating she could be
> In conversations of the heart!
> . . . .
> Avoid her! there's no heart in her! (250)

At the same time this technique acts to set off this "new Medea" from the crowds of other beauties. Nina, like the others, is "surrounded" by a circle of young men; unlike the others she is also "surrounded" by a demoniac circle of "passionate contagion," which sweetly infects the air on all sides.

Her lover, Arseny, displays even more of the traits of the traditional Byronic hero; he is solitary, filled with secret reflections and
strange behavior. He carries on his brow "The traces of torment-
ing passions / The traces of distressed reflections" (252). Too, he
has made restless trips to foreign lands in search of distraction. But
beneath the cold weariness and the "dismal carelessness" of his
exterior, he has preserved a reservoir of sensitivity, characteristic of
his type.

Apart from its characters "The Ball" has certain other affinities
with Pushkin's works; as in "Evgeny Onegin," for example, each of
the forty-six stanzas in "The Ball" contains fourteen lines, although
Baratynsky employs a different rhyming pattern.[14] "The Ball" is
Baratynsky's only long poem divided into stanzas of equal length,
and—like all his others—it is written in iambic tetrameter. As is
usual in both his lyrics and longer poems, a high level of exact rhyme
is preserved; however, *slugá—ruká*, occurring in the thirtieth
stanza can be regarded as a lapse in quality.

The structure of "The Ball" shows more originality than its plot.
It opens with the description of a Moscow ball, during which the
Princess Nina causes a stir by leaving suddenly in the middle of a
quadrille. An extended flashback recreates the story of her overpow-
ering love for Arseny, of an "enchantress" now herself "enchanted"
by the ambiguous personality of a stranger. Dismayed by his constant melancholy, she discovers that he, through jealousy, has
abandoned a childhood love, Olga. At this point the Lensky-Onegin
parallel becomes especially obvious. He eventually abandons Nina,
as well, but later sends her a letter telling of a renewal of his former
happiness with Olga.

The movement of the plot is resumed when Nina deserts the ball
which Arseny and Olga have attended. Here, the author again reveals his technical skill and dexterity with recurrent terminology;
the transition back to the main thread of the action—the ball—is
smoothed by recurrence of the same expressions with which it was
first described. Nina returns to her bedroom to poison herself, and
the poem closes with a brief account of her funeral.

During the course of the narrative Arseny's Byronic pose disin-
tegrates: his appearance and speeches of the first part hardly harmonize with the sentimental story of his love for Olga and the excessively
emotional tone of his letter. Nina, however, remains true to form,
and the all-embracing nature of a disposition given to absolutes is
repeatedly emphasized by use of the word *polnyy* ("filled with,"

"absolute"), which also traces and highlights the crucial stages of her psychological drama:

> Filled with defiance for opinion...
>
> ....
>
> Filled with a passionate oblivion,
> Filled with the bliss of new existence...
>
> ....
>
> "You'll be my absolute sovereign."
>
> ....
>
> To no avail, and filled with sorrow... (249, 253, 254, 258)

The detailed and psychologized account of her preparation for the ball represents a move toward a Realistic plane, as does the description of her face caught in death: "On it the hasty course of death; / The eyes stand wide and the mouth in foam..." (263).

The concise, yet incisive sketch of Nina's husband, the prince, is likewise imbued with an air of prosaic factuality. The character of this card-playing, "not very sentimental" man, depicted blowing his nose as he enters Nina's room, is perhaps elucidated best in his detached reaction to the death: "The prince, without especial pain, / His fate committed to God's will" (264).

The satirical treatment of the setting—the fashionable society world of Moscow—constitutes another manifestation of Realism. The satire here is sharper than in "Feasts" and more penetrating. The picture of old ladies in the first stanza, "with a dead smile on the lips" (248), is a motif that was to receive a much more extended development by later Russian writers, including Gogol and Blok. And the long string of coaches that appears for the ball in the beginning turns up just as dutifully for the funeral in the conclusion.

As "Eda," "The Ball" brought on a mixed reaction in the literary press. Much of the negative criticism accused Baratynsky of immorality in regard to the figure of Nina and of imitative work. Pushkin, however, was again favorably impressed; he wrote in 1828 on "Baratynsky's 'The Ball'": "This brilliant work is filled with original delights and unusual charm. The poet with astonishing skill has combined in a fast-moving story a witty and impassioned tone, metaphysics, and poetry."[15]

Kireevsky disagreed: "In Baratynsky's 'The Ball' [*Balnyy vecher*] there is no focus for feeling and (if one may speak of poetry in the language of mechanics) there is not one *component force* in it, in which all emotional trends could have become united and balanced."[16]

"The Ball" is, without doubt, rich in its diversity of tonalities and portraiture. But once again, as in "Eda," Baratynsky proved to be incapable of introducing any real harmony, any "component force," into the poem as a whole. Thus it is that the convincingly Realistic depictions, while successful in themselves, fail to find any common meeting point with the more lyrical and Romantic episodes. In a similar way the lurid circumstances of Nina's death, while consistent with her frenetic personality, are handled in places with a somewhat unnecessary melodrama, which is at odds with those instances where they receive a more Realistic treatment.

In brief, Baratynsky was unable to project a sustained Romanticist perspective into his poem. His literary temperament, having some fragmented affinity with Byron and, in this sense, with Pushkin, could not assimilate enough of the Romantic spirit that was required for an extended work. He felt closer perhaps to the Classical genre of the didactic tale.

IV *The Gypsy Girl*

In spite of the Romanticism of separate motifs and ideas which were becoming more evident in Baratynsky's verse toward the end of the 1820's, he still desired to make a name for himself in the genre of the Romantic long poem—a goal which had eluded him in "Eda" and "The Ball." This desire resulted in the last and most ambitious of his long poems, "The Gypsy Girl" (*Tsyganka*), which first appeared in full in 1831 under the title "The Concubine" (*Nalozhnitsa*). In November of 1829 he had written to Kireevsky: "...I have a new poem in the works, an ultraromantic poem."[17]

The characters of this "ultraromantic" work resemble, in many ways, those of "The Ball." Eletsky is more developed than Arseny, however, and his Byronic, Onegin-like break with society is at once more complete and more psychologically motivated. He has disappeared from the stifling drawing rooms to establish his own depraved code of action in foreign countries. Having returned to Moscow, as a decisive blow to whatever of his reputation he may have retained, he takes the Gypsy girl, Sara, into his home in order to fill his still-existent inner vacuum.

Even in the depths of corruption and degeneracy, though, Eletsky has remained susceptible to the "better inspirations" and has preserved within himself the traditional reserves of emotion and sensitivity. These emerge when, amidst the noise and bustle of an

Easter fair, he sees a young lady of Moscow society, Vera Volkhov-skaya, whose idealized image recalls that of both Eda and Olga.

As Arseny had been caught between Nina and Olga, Eletsky becomes trapped between Sara and Vera. Yet another similarity to "The Ball" is the flashback, represented in "The Gypsy Girl" by the second chapter, which recreates Eletsky's past and describes his first meeting with Vera. That and several subsequent meetings were of the eyes only; employing recurrent terminology and psychological epithets, the poet pinpoints the initial stages of their love in this motion of the eyes. This basic Symbolist device, which expresses an inner sentiment through an action, had been effectively used in "Eda."

In much the same way Baratynsky uses gestures to indicate, on the one hand, the movement of the plot, and, on the other, the parallel development of the psychological dilemma. For example, Vera's departure from the fair is noted: "Her friend, esteemed, advanced in years,/Extends his arm to the young maid" (280). The respectable old man is her guardian-uncle, and the action conveys a suggestion of her innocent and sheltered existence. On a late July afternoon on the Tverskoy Boulevard, another hand is extended to Vera, this time to offer her the inevitably dropped glove: "And hastily he lifted it. / Extended it to her" (281). Here the hand is Eletsky's and the same silent motion as that recorded in the previous occurrence has dramatically different overtones.

As Eletsky leaves a masquerade ball, where he and Vera have at last spoken with each other, Sara unexpectedly appears, and Vera has a third hand lifted in her direction:

> Before him was another face,
> It glittered with embittered eyes,
> With savagely uplifted arm
> It threatened Vera, disappeared
> Behind the crowd with Eletsky. (285)

It is this concrete interplay of eyes and hands that gives visible indications of the developing conflict among the three main characters in "The Gypsy Girl." All the physical impact of the clash between the two women, made striking by the lack of verbal communication between them, is focused and symbolized in this single scene; they do not see each other again.

The fourth chapter concentrates on Sara, whose primitive nature is perhaps best reflected in her colorful language. She poses a threat to Vera, but she herself is threatened by the possibility of being discarded. The essence of her conversation with Eletsky represents a carry-over of ideas that had characterized his own melodramatic speech to Vera at the ball: she obliges him, as he would like to oblige Vera. His words to the contrary, Sara knows that in the end he will reject her and that she will be "swept aside, like trash."

In the meantime winter has arrived. Pouring rains become frost; waters freeze over, and a snow storm twists among the ponds and bare trees. The transformation of the quiet summer moon into the turbulent blizzards of winter acquires a sobering accent in retrospect and sets the tone for the conclusion, where the mutual fascination of Eletsky and Vera destroys the one and creates a living death for the other. It is perhaps significant that the storm forms a recurrent image, which subsequently appears at moments of high dramatic tension.

Moreover, the development of Vera's love is described directly in terms of nature:

> The youthful maiden did not know,
> Being filled with happiness,
> . . . .
> That this congenial little breeze,
> Caressing her so lightly was,—
> The prophet of a ruinous storm. . . . (293)

Vera, as Eda, did not realize until it was too late that a breath of the breeze would be disastrous, that finally it would devastate her life. Vera's decisive capitulation to her passions is also reminiscent of Eda.

Sara, in the interim, driven to near frenzy by her grief, resorts to witchcraft in order to reclaim her man; an old Gypsy woman comes in from the swirling snow to give her a glass of wine containing a love potion, which is actually a poison. Eletsky himself then appears and announces his plans to leave that evening with Vera. Having given him the wine, Sara is unable to resist reproaches, which are delivered in a language imbued with coarse, colloquial peculiarities and graphic imagery:

> And I . . . what tears I have poured forth,
> What outrages have I not swallowed,
> Preserving an embittered silence!
> You ceased to love, but I still loved;

You drove me unrelentingly—
I fawned upon you, wicked one,
Just like a bitch. Examine me
A little closer: say to me,
Did I fall to your lot like this?
My eyes have faded from my tears;
My face has shrunk, my breast dried up;
I have done everything but croak! . . . (303)

This episode is psychologically convincing: Sara, thinking she will regain his love, has unknowingly murdered him.

In the moonless night Vera waits futilely, enveloped by the screaming wind, which in its ferocity lifts the still rampaging snow to the rooftops. In the end all is statically quiet. Eletsky sleeps in indifference, and grass and snow continue to cover him unconcernedly. Passions have subsided in Vera, but so have the joy and sense of existence. Sara pays for her passion with insanity.

Eletsky has within himself the bifurcation typical of the lyrical hero in much of Baratynsky's shorter verse; his reason had matured "in the very experience of passions"; further, he is often oppressed by "heavy, black thoughts." Of the alternative reasons possibly responsible for Vera's subsequent loss of interest in living, one is set forth almost didactically: her intellect has shown her the "madness" of love and romantic fantasies.

In "Eda," "The Ball" and "The Gypsy Girl" passions are discredited and lead to death. In the latter two of these, they lead to crime, as well. In the brief lyric which Baratynsky dedicated to his sister-in-law upon completion of "The Ball," "On the Sending of 'The Ball' to S. E." (*Pri posylke "Bala" S. E.*), 1828, he referred to the "criminal heat of worthless passions." Another lyric dating from 1824, "Love" (*Lyubov*), which portrays the destructive force of love, could well have served as the preface to all three of these Romantic poems.

"The Gypsy Girl's" 1209 lines make it almost twice as long as "Eda" and "The Ball." Unlike these, it is divided into chapters (eight), which has the effect of lending additional direction and order to the exposition and consequent movement to the dramatic subject matter. Its rhyme, which observes no constant pattern, is, in general, richer than that of the two earlier works. In places, however, the rhyme *Véra—méra* ("measure") takes on a certain monotony; and in the final version of the poem, the word *rasstavanie* ("parting") is left dangling without a partner.

Baratynsky accompanied "The Gypsy Girl" with a preface, which, as in the case of "Eda," was intended to forestall criticism before it arose. Using mostly Classical references, he defends the moral right of the poet to depict vice, so long as he depicts it fairly: "From this it follows, that moral criticism of a literary work is restricted to the simple analysis: are its representations just or unjust? Criticism may complain, as well, of their incompleteness, for the most complete description of the subject matter is at the same time the truest" (322).

Accordingly, rather than demand positive moral enlightenment from literature, he professes to see in it "a science, similar to other sciences" and to seek in it "knowledge, and nothing else": "I know, that one may seek the beautiful in it, but the beautiful is not for everyone; it is incomprehensible even to people who are intelligent, but not gifted with special sensitiveness: not everyone can read with feeling, each can read with curiosity" (321).

The critics were almost unanimous in condemning "The Gypsy Girl." Only the article of Kireevsky [18] and that of the friendly *Literary Gazette*[19] were affirmative. Pushkin, in a letter to Pletnyov, called it a "marvel,"[20] but even so close a friend as Zhukovsky objected to its original title, "The Concubine."[21] The unexplained poison brought by the old Gypsy woman troubled Belinsky.[22]

Perhaps the most caustic response of all belonged to the critic N. Nadezhdin, who attacked both the poem and the ideas expressed in the preface. After pointing out that Baratynsky did not understand the difference between belles-lettres and literature, in general, he proceeded to demonstrate that the poet's depictions were neither fair nor complete. Finally, he quite accurately asserted that the poetic justice against which Baratynsky had armed himself in the preface was observed rather severely in the poem.[23]

This article induced Baratynsky to publish a rare defense of his work[24] in which he again failed to make that distinction between artistic literature and other types of literature, which Nadezhdin had spoken of and which was so important in Schelling's esthetic conceptions of beauty and truth in art. He himself felt this shortcoming, and upon sending his article to Kireevsky for approval, he wrote: "Look over my anticriticism, and discard whatever seems to you superfluous. I fear that I do not adhere to the German dogma in it and that some heresies have stolen into it."[25]

Despite his defense, Baratynsky set about making major changes in his work. In the version which he prepared for the 1835 edition of his poetry, he replaced the title "The Concubine," which had been disagreeable to so many, with "The Gypsy Girl," and also eliminated the preface. In his 1842 revision he disposed of an entire chapter (the original Chapter IV) and compressed certain episodes.

But his reputation was already wrecked and the appearance of the poem marked a significant milestone in the continuing fall of his popularity. He took relatively little interest in the content of "The Gypsy Girl" as such, as is made clear by an excerpt from his letter of June, 1831 to Kireevsky: "Usually my latest work seems to me worse than the previous ones, but rereading 'The Concubine,' the lightness and verity of its style in comparison with my previous poems always impresses me."[26]

This concern with style, with a corresponding absence of attention to the "ultraromanticism" of its theme and character portrayals, was responsible, in large part, for the failure of the work. The same lack of synthesis and balance that penetrates "Eda" and "The Ball" is even more apparent here. At odds with the fanciful plot with its Naturalistic details and sensational motif of poison are the Realistically exact descriptions of the background against which it is worked out. The character profiles pose an unresolved conflict with the convincing psychological techniques applied in their development.

Apart from these irreconcilable tendencies in method, "The Gypsy Girl," as well as "Eda" and "The Ball," suffer from inevitable comparison with Pushkin's long poems and it is probably true that they "would never have been written without the example of Pushkin."[27] In the final analysis, despite the unmistakable artistic merits of certain of their separate parts—and, in this respect, of "The Gypsy Girl," especially—Baratynsky's experiments did not have a substantial influence on the development of the Romantic poem in Russia.[28] The genre as a whole continued to be beyond the limits of his fundamentally intellectualist perspectives, and, consequently, remained essentially alien to his poetic mentality.

CHAPTER 4

The Conflict Between Reality
and a Higher Realm

THE middle and late 1820's were a period of perplexed transition in both Baratynsky's creative development and his personal life. In April, 1825, he was promoted to lieutenant *(poruchik)* which, insofar as his verse was concerned, deprived him of the image of the "exile." Moreover, in October of the same year he arrived in Moscow on leave and did not return to Finland, thus putting an effective end to the inspiration and background provided by the special character of Finnish nature.

Although his marriage in 1826 strengthened his ties with Moscow, he continued to feel somewhat alienated in the city. This situation contributed in lending an indefinable fascination to the years spent in Finland, and he came to look upon them as a time of youth and friendship. His physical isolation notwithstanding, he had been an integral part of the animated literary life of Petersburg.

It was also in Finland that his fame as a poet, and, in particular, as the "poet of Finland," had spread; and this, too, cast a spell of illusive appeal over the period. Even after he left, a certain elegiac mood of lonesomeness and solitude, intensified as a result of the stay there, endured in his poetry. In another sense his work was never again to convey the tones of unaffected simplicity and confidence implicit in such poems as "Finland" and the first epistle to Gnedich.

Life was now filled with new realities. His first attempt to create an original trend in the genre of the long poem was essentially unsuccessful. At one time he was to consider abandoning poetry altogether and turning to prose. Toward the end of 1831 he finished the only known example of his artistic prose, the tale "The Signet Ring" *(Persten)*. Simultaneously he was working both on a play and on a projected biography of Delvig, neither of which has been preserved.

In the meantime, however, even within his own circle of literary friends, he was still accused of being a "Frenchman" and a "marquis." In 1825, for example, he found himself protesting in a letter to Pushkin: "Don't think that I am a marquis to such an extent as not to feel the beauties of romantic tragedy."[1] The time had clearly come for a new direction in the approach to poetic creativity.

I *The Literary Implications of Schelling's Idealism*

Soon after his marriage, Baratynsky became acquainted with that circle of writers, philosophers, and literary critics known as the "Wisdom-lovers" *(Lyubomudry).* This was a Romanticist group which drew its principal sources of inspiration from Schelling. As regards the specifically literary implications of Schelling's idealistic philosophical system, it may be asserted in brief that he elevated poetry to the status of philosophy, and attempted to synthesize these with religion and myth.

He [Schelling] put forward the grandiose claim that the idea of beauty, taken in the higher Platonic sense "unites all other ideas." "I am convinced," he says, "that the highest act of reason is the esthetic act embracing all ideas and that truth and goodness are made kindred only in beauty. The philospher must have as much esthetic power as the poet. Poetry thus assumes a new dignity; it becomes what it was in the beginning—the teacher of mankind: for there is no philosophy or history any more; poetry alone will outlive all other sciences and arts."[2]

The poet becomes a herald of truth and the act of creation becomes an occult process in which subjectivity merges with reality:

Art thus breaks down the barriers between the real and the ideal world. It is the representation of the infinite, a union of nature and freedom, for it is both a product of the conscious and the unconscious, of the imagination which unconsciously creates our real world and consciously creates the ideal world of art.[3]

Related to this idea is Schelling's connection of art with nature, which, in turn, is linked with the creative consciousness. Art forms a parallel with nature and its creative power, and in expressing the essence of nature, it seeks to emulate this creative power.[4] In his conception of apprehension through artistic imagination, Schelling necessarily rejected the faculty of reason, perceived in the rationalistic sense.

Baratynsky became familiar with Schelling through his contacts with the Wisdom-lovers and, particularly, through his special rapport with Kireevsky. Exposure to these ideas began at a time when, as mentioned, he was experiencing a transitional period, a time when his creative perspectives were far from clear. Separated both from Finland and from the proximity of his Petersburg literary ties, and criticized for his adherence to French Classicism, he stood on a kind of crossway and welcomed the opportunity to explore Schelling's concepts through his Moscow friends.

However, it is important to remember that Baratynsky never actually accepted Schelling's philosophical system. His position in 1826, reflected in a letter to Pushkin, never substantially changed: "Now knowing German, I was glad of a chance to get acquainted with German esthetics. It has a poetry all its own which is pleasing, but its principles, it seems to me, may be refuted philosophically."[5] His preoccupation with reason and his training in French rationalism did not permit him to accept the fundamental irrationalism of Schelling's system. On the other hand, he was susceptible to its "poetry," which began to influence certain motifs and themes of many of his most characteristic poems during the second half of the 1820's.

II *Poetry as a Motif of Escape*

The esthetic teachings of the Wisdom-lovers were concerned with poetic originality and the secretive, highly individual essence of the creative act itself. This group of Baratynsky's lyrics, written between 1828 and 1834, reflects these concerns and includes some of his best verse.

The theme of poetry and the poet first appeared in his work as early as 1827 in "The Last Death" and in "To°°°" *(K°°°)*; in the latter the poet is referred to as "teacher and prophet." But the grand calling of the poetic mission received a more forthright working-out in "Do not imitate: genius is original . . ." *(Ne podrazhay: svoeobrazen geniy . . .)*, 1828, in which Mickiewicz is advised: "Arise, arise and recall: yourself, you are a god!" (137).

Baratynsky turns to this theme again in another poem directed against imitators, "To Imitators" *(Podrazhatelyam)*, 1829. The introductory lines are reminiscent of the epilogue to "The Transmigration of Souls," but the motif of distress acting as an impetus to inspiration is developed with overtones that it lacked earlier. The poet's suffering acquires an aura of mystery, accentuated by the original compound adjective *dushemutitelnyy* ("anguished," "agonized"). Racked by misery, he projects his pain into a celestial framework where it becomes a mark of divinity, of the "highest powers." For the expression of these powers, he pays with frenzied inner convulsions, but his own transfiguration follows as a natural result. His face encircled with "imperishable" rays, he becomes a god on earth; he speaks to mortals with the voice of heaven.

Conversely, those whose sufferings are borrowed, those who cry out with an "affected howl" are held up to ridicule and scorn. The contrast is sharply etched and in the conclusion, the coarse muse of the imitators is reduced to a depraved beggar, imploring alms for "another's" child. Religious and archaic terminology gives way here to an appropriately colloquial tonality.

"A wondrous city at times emerges..." (*Chudnyy grad poroy solyotsya...*), 1829, represents a further elaboration on the Schelling-like elevation of poetry, whereby commonplace reality clashes with that higher world of harmony. This brief poem is evenly structured on an extended simile, but in reverse order from the usual.[6] In ordinary poetic practice after words such as "thus," the image is developed figuratively. Here, the first sentence-quatrain, which contains the metaphorical "city" emerging from the clouds, precedes "thus" (*tak*), whereas the second sentence-quatrain presents the corresponding statement in the literal sense: "Thus ephemeral creations/Of poetic fantasy/Disappear at a breath/Of an alien vanity" (141).

The exalted "city" of poetry, whose existence is emphasized by the location of *chudnyy* ("wondrous") as the first word and the sole word in first-foot position in this trochaic lyric to receive a strong stress, came essentially from Schelling and his partisans. But the basic elements of this theme, expressed in the cult of art, can be found in Baratynsky's own verse as early as 1820. Despairing of finding order in his contradictory reality, the poet turns to poetry, but his beautiful city is swept away by a "breath" of prosaic actuality as quickly as it takes shape.

Even that fleeting glimpse of harmony accorded by poetry is rejected in "When I was young, with ringing call..." (*Byvalo, otrok, zvonkim klikom...*), 1831. This poem, which concluded Baratynsky's collection of 1835, is at once indicative of his overall dejection and lack of poetic prospects. As much of his work during this time, it provides an example of Romantic content subordinated to Classical precision in form.

Two unconnected concepts are linked together in the poem and synthesized into a unified whole. The first of these, a forest echo, is treated in the first quatrain: a boy is fascinated by the response to his own voice. In these four lines the alternating feminine-masculine rhyming vowel is a constant "i." The second concept is an extended analogy of the first: a youth is charmed by the rhymes of his poetry, wherein sounds respond to one another in the same way as the echo had answered the shout. These six lines reveal two consecutive feminine rhymes twice followed by a masculine, but the previous "i" is gradually overcome by the more mellifluous "a," in the same way as rhyme itself had succeeded the echo in the forest:

> Porá drugáya nastupíla,
> I rífma yúnoshu pleníla,
> Lesnóe ékho zamenyá.
> Igrá stikhóv, igrá zlatáya!
> Kak zvúki, zvúkam otvecháya,
> Byválo, nézhili menyá! (147)

Another season came to pass, / And rhyme in turn beguiled the youth, The forest echo substituting. / The play of verse, the golden play! / How sounds, responding thus to sounds, / Used to afford me solace then!

But as the first amusement had lost its appeal, so does the second; and the alternating feminine-masculine pattern makes a reappearance in the last quatrain, in which the rhyming "a" of poetry is matched with an invading "o": the euphonic harmony of both the echo and poetry disappears, as the poet renounces each in turn:

> No vsyó prokhódit. Ostyváyu
> Ya i k garmónii stikhóv—
> I kak dubróv ne oklikáyu,
>
> Tak ne ishchú sozvúchnykh slóv. (147)

But all goes by. And I grow cold / Even to harmony of verse—/ And I no longer call to groves / Nor search for euphony in words.

This resolution to the two previous passages delineates more sharply the symbolic correspondence between the echo and the rhyme. The euphony of rhyme is superimposed upon the euphony of the forest echo; the harmony of poetry is identified with the harmony of nature. The Schelling idea of art forming a parallel with nature is realized in a distinctly symmetrical poetic structure. But the poet is unable to accept this harmony for his own, and his rejection of it is indicative of deep-seated discord.

In a reversal of this mood, poetic harmony is accepted in the poem, "In days of boundless enthusiasms..." *(V dni bezgranichnykh uvlecheniy...)*, 1831. The first part is composed of twelve lines, half of which deal with the "unrestrained passions" of youth. Opposed to these is the "ideal of beautiful proportionalities" (second six lines), implicit in the "measured verses of the poet" (152), which coexisted within him during the days of wildest turmoil. When one element of the poetic temperament craved the chaos of frenzied sensation, it was saved by the ideal of the other element.

As before, two principles struggle for dominance in the divided personality; this time, passions are sublimated and reconciled in a higher order. The word "proportionalities" *(sorazmernosti)*, rarely used in the plural, suggests the influence of Kireevsky, who in a critical article of the same year, had written that Baratynsky's poetry "breathes uniquely with love of proportionalities and harmony."[7]

The concluding stanza projects the model of inner harmony into all of life. As in the first part, the transience and agitation of passions are contrasted with the "laws of eternal beauty" (152) manifested in poetry. Expressed here is Schelling's conception of the idea of beauty, and consequently, of the esthetic act, functioning as the unifying force of all ideas and all of existence. In his trancelike status the poet sees the "vast outline of a poetic world" (152) in much the same fashion as he had envisioned a "wondrous city" of poetry in the other poem.

The traces of Schelling's influence are integrated effectively within the trends of Baratynsky's own poetic ideas. Earlier his boundless thought in its search for limitation had come to rest on the underworld of death ("Death," 1828), whose "harmony" *(soglasie)* was imposed on the turbulence of existence. Here it is the lyre, symbol of a higher realm, which provides the same "harmony" for boundless passions. This predilection for extremes was the reflection of a poetic personality torn apart by a struggle between contradictions.

The first of the two epistles dedicated to Yazykov in 1831, "To N. M. Yazykov" *(N. M. Yazykovu)*, depicts the same disunion of a personality gravitating towards opposites. The conflict is one be-

tween passions and sobering experience rather than between passions and a thirst for higher harmony. The theme of withdrawal from
"wild passions," of submission to the lessons of experience and of
consequent immersion in "decent reflections"—present in early epistles—is emphasized by the repeated occurrence of "when"
(kogda). However, in the lines immediately following these, the
poet affirms an outlook signifying the presence of a contradictory
attitude: "But then I like the daring rapture,/The rakish ardor of
your verse" (152).

But, as if the muse must some day atone for these ecstasies, he
forecasts that his friend will become "the poet of another happiness": "And you'll yourself before the world/Redeem the pranks
of your young muse" (153).

In the second of these epistles "To Yazykov" *(Yazykovu)*, the
poet's muse is a diety, who poses a sharp variance to the vulgar
crowd surrounding her. In evidence here is an example of that
complex syntactic construction which was later to become characteristic of Baratynsky: *Oná rugálas chúdnoy dévy / Ey neponyát-
nym bozhestvóm* ("Of the wondrous maiden it abused / The
deity obscure to it") (153). Her features stand out in concrete
detail, and instead of awaiting expiation for her sins, she is pictured
as "high-born," a "tsarina" with "majestic gaze."

At this point the poet's double attitude acquires a distinct clarity. In "On the Sending of 'The Ball' to S.E." passion is depicted as
"unworthy" and even "criminal," and it takes on a similar connota-
tion in the previous epistle. Here it shines with a "worthy brilliance"
and is deserving of the "diadem and purple." But passion is allied
with poetry in this instance and the muse is elevated to a godhead;
and she takes her passion with her, to achieve synthesis and harmony, there, in her lofty dominions.

But that higher world is an inconstant entity and in "When will
the darkness disappear . . ." *(Kogda ischeznet omrachenie . . .)*,
1834, the poet fails to evoke it even for a moment. Entangled in
"meshes" of bewildering thought, he embodies his condition in a
malignant "demon," who throws over his spirit a numbing sleep.
Contrasted with the blackness of this inner deadlock is the bright-
ness of a remote "all-illuminating day," realized through inspiration.
Paralyzed by the demon, he is unable to lose himself in the secret
ritual of poetic creation or—its parallel, according to Schelling—
to "embrace nature."

The second part continues the preponderance of rhymed "e's"

and "a's" of the first, as well as the latter's string of rhetorical questions and its emphasis on distinctly visual impressions of inspiration as opposed to the darkness of the poet's present state:

> In vain, the pleas? in vain, reproaches?
> Shall I see again your canopies,
> Gardens of sacred poetry?
> Shall I see you, its luminaries?
> In vain! I feel: the grave
> Has accepted me alive,
> And smothering my lightsome gift,
> Upon my bosom, fatal thought
> Is lying like a burial mound. (164)

The finality of the negative response is underscored by recurrence of "in vain" (*votshche*), whereas the third line above in the original (*Sadý poézii svyatóy*) acquires intensity as a result of its unrhymed "oy." The heavenly gardens of poetry and their celestial luminaries, now strikingly distant, are antithetical to the living grave into which he has lowered himself.

"Fatal thought," that perpetual absorption with the paradoxes of reality, has smothered not only the internal accessibility to self-oblivion, but also the spontaneity of being. The effect is more severe than the abdication of desires and hope counseled by the figure of "Truth," who at the very least proffered an impassive peace. Incapable of either accepting that rational truth or of giving himself to his passions, the poet is pinned between the one and the other, and the end result is a swirling and deadening maze of endless reflection, from which escape is impossible.

Yet the mystical essence of poetic inspiration does afford him a respite in "Poetry heals an ailing spirit..." (*Bolyashchiy dukh vrachuet pesnopenie...*), 1834. The deliverance that is yearned for in the previous poem is achieved to the extent that dejection appears as a "painful delusion." Not only is he lifted above that dejection, but passions are integrated in a transcendent symphony of accord. Purged of the debilitating effects of dissension and incompatibility, the spirit is communicant to an undefiled and ethereal realm of harmony and tranquility.

The disturbed questioning and intonation of the iambic tetrameter in "When will the darkness disappear..." are transformed here into a smoothly flowing and relaxed pentameter; and the unstable and inconsistent nature of the rhymed "e's" and "a's" which formed a majority in that lyric dominate here in an orderly pattern.

Enduring consistency in disposition, even within a narrow realm of experience, was not characteristic of Baratynsky's poetic personality. If it is clear that much of his work during these years drew its inspiration from a Romantically idealistic conception of poetry and the poet, it is also clear that during the same period, he relied to an equal or greater extent on the incapacity to envision that ideal. In this sense he lost the opportunity to establish for his poetry an affirmative outlook.

III *The Vision of Death*

The focal point of inspiration in these poems, as opposed to the preceding works, is provided by the lower world of death. But in frequent efforts to transcend that inspiration, a higher place embodying stability and eternity, and at times connected with a religious motif, also appears. The influence of Schelling is less marked, but nevertheless present in various reflections.

One of Baratynsky's first works in which certain ideas of Schelling are obvious is "The Last Death" (*Poslednyaya smert*), 1827. An essay on the future, it is composed of eight twelve-line stanzas, each of which follows an identical rhyming pattern. Its solemn and heavy iambic pentameter, with the caesura after the fourth syllable, blends with an elevated intonation which connects it with a previous series of poems, including "Two Fates" and "The Skull." Like these, "The Last Death" is distinguished by consistent development of thought in generalized terms. Unlike these, it is based on a vision, a device peculiar to Romanticism.

Reminiscent of Schelling is the description of the creative condition, the state of " being" (*bytie*). The poet is experiencing a profound absorption, as if he were suspended between sleep and waking, consciousness and unconsciousness, a condition in which "comprehension verges on madness" (129). He is midway between dream and reality. Being in full control of his senses, he is at the same time assailed by visions, so that the ultimate psychological result is likened to the elemental turmoil of an "ancient motherland" of chaos. Use of the epithet *davnyaya* ("ancient") struck the reader of the 1820's with a pronounced overtone, as later Tyutchev's "native chaos" (*rodimyy khaos*) had a similar effect. Further, the simile "waves," used in connection with "visions," is, by dint of its concrete delineation, suggestive of the sea—never mentioned directly.

The correspondence between the primeval chaos of nature and a responsive element in the poetic mentality links "The Last Death" with "The Waterfall" and "The Storm." But the consequence of this particular state of mind—a vision—again recalls the ideas of Schelling. More characteristic of Baratynsky is that the poet is unable to determine the specific source of this vision and debates whether it be a product of his imagination or his intellect.

The future, with its swirling events and epochs, begins to assume form, but the mystical atmosphere is preserved and intensified by a description which parallels that in the introductory lines: such is the cataclysmic flight of poetic fancy, however, that the sea gives way to the clouds. The following couplet, concluding the second stanza, indicates a full shift to substantiality, as the vision attains stability: "And then at last I saw without a cover/The final fate of everything alive" (130).

The next two stanzas, which represent the highest point in concentration of visual imagery, are an account of a world rich in artistic and material achievements. The forces of reason have prevailed and even the elements have submitted to their sway. The "rebellious whirlpools of the seas" have been settled with artificial islands and the skies are crisscrossed by man-made wings. The "enemies" of enlightenment have been put to shame and compelled to reeducate themselves during this "splendid feast of reason." Supporting the theme of a triumphant rationality and lending it a marching solemnity is the accumulation of Church Slavonic terminology, laid out in equally concentrated rhythmic-syntactic uniformity.

At this point a second vision appears to the poet, who marvels at the scope of human progress. Centuries have passed. Anticipating yet further accomplishments, he is dismayed by what he sees. Humanity, having the advantages of a phenomenal standard of living, leads an increasingly intellectual life. Physical pursuits are shunned, and the high degree of excellence in development of the brain is offset by degeneration of the body. Marriages are barren, and reason itself eventually succumbs to fantasy: "And living thought on wings was taking them/Into chaos and to the empyrean" (131). Thus Baratynsky follows his considerations to their logical and extreme conclusion. Thought, depicted in a submerged metaphor, is personified and made tangible, and the realm of abstract processes is again joined to that of immediate experience.

The final sweeping tableau is but a continuation of this unbending line of reasoning. Death, personified and all-engulfing, is omnipresent, and the noise and commotion of civilization are slowly reduced to the eerie cries of livestock, crazed by hunger. In the end all is majestically quiet and motionless; only the fog whirling over the deserted landscape lies beneath the sun. Nature, as if avenging itself and cleansing itself of impurity, overwhelms human rationality and resumes its ancient ascendancy over the earth. The effect is given an added impression of pagan and primitive splendor by the rare use of the attributive *dikaya* ("savage") with the *porfira* ("purple") of nature.

This outcome is close to Schelling's conception of the poet as the "liberator of nature."[8] In discrediting reason, however, Baratynsky reaches the same judgment he had reached in "Truth" and other poems. It is in this connection that "The Last Death" represents a new and independent variation on an old theme and reveals, as well, the continuing preoccupation with death and extermination.

As earlier works, it shows a typically logical development of subject matter. The first two of its eight stanzas comprise the prelude and are decidedly Romantic in tone and content. The next two pertain to the golden epoch of reason, whereas the fifth and sixth are concerned with its excessive expansion. The closing stanzas describe dissolution and death. Lending an additional consistency to this analytical structure is the distinct separation and simultaneous introduction of each visionary era by recurrence of analogous vocabulary and syntax, i.e., *Proshlí veká. Yasnét ochám moím* ("Centuries passed. Appear before my eyes") (130), *Proshlí veká, i tút moím ochám* ("Centuries passed, and here before my eyes") (131). This extended symmetrical structure is in contrast to the Romanticist device of the vision, which receives thereby a logical treatment; it is also implicitly contradicted by the rejection of reason in the conclusion.

In theme and composition "The Last Death" harmonizes with previous trends of Baratynsky's artistic evolution in spite of the apparent influence of Schelling, which is integrated effectively within these trends. On the other hand, in subject matter and in specific details it constitutes one of the first examples in the tradition of Russian antiutopian and apocalyptic literature, and it is in this way that Baratynsky transcends his former range of both imagination and originality.

If "The Last Death" can be seen as a manifestation of a troubled intellectual actuality, then "Death" *(Smert)*, 1828,—which became a favorite of Tolstoy—attempts by a process involving sublimation and justification, to come to terms with it. Unlike the earlier work, in which death is the result of an internal order, it is depicted here as a necessary link in the chain of biological events, as a necessary condition to life itself. This factor places "Death" in that line of Baratynsky's poetry which is characterized by a deterministic approach and which includes such diverse poems as "Dejection" and "The Skull."

Further, its elevated thematics, characteristic of the Wisdom-lovers, and its oratorical tonality, expressed, in particular, in use of obsolete diction, associate it stylistically with another series of his poems. These are distinguished, as well, by projection of personal preoccupations into a universal framework. The archaisms in "Death," however, are not merely the conventional archaisms of the time, but include terminology which was practically unintelligible to the average reader; this tendency is illustrated by such words as the Church Slavonic "*dshcher*" ("daughter") and the Old Russian *prya* ("quarrels").

The pervasive atmosphere of "Truth," where the poet cringed before the lamp of knowledge, is evoked in the first stanza by the use of "servile" *(rabolepnyy)*:

> Death I'll not call the daughter of dark
> And, in a servile fantasy
> Granting it a ghastly skeleton,
> I'll not equip it with a scythe. (134)

Here he grapples with the same problem on a higher level, but reveals an opposite attitude: he has learned the "impassivity" he rejected before. Recalling the image of Truth is the exalted image of Death, which, like Truth, unifies the sphere of purely abstract ideas with that of material things. Death, instead of the traditional skeleton armed with a scythe, becomes a "holy virgin," who, carrying the olive branch of peace, caresses with the same hand both the master and the slave.

As in "The Skull" the poet attempts to penetrate to the essence of death. Unlike that earlier attempt, which dissolved into a rationalization of the status quo, he arrives at a formal explanation which takes on all the attributes of a cult. In a vast portrayal which

extends from the timeless elemental anarchy preceding the beginnings of creation to the "condition of our troubled days" (135),
death is presented as the universal pacifier, subduing the "turbulence of existence."

"Existence" (*bytie*), apart from its literal import, refers, on
another plane, to the turbulent reality of the poet's thought processes and is immediately suggestive of the opening of "The Last
Death." In this connection the boundless sweep of nature
imagery in "Death" becomes symbolic of the range of that thought;
in its thirst for limitation, for some semblance of stability, it rests
on death. In this context each image and verb acquire a double significance, in which active participles reinforce the impression of
motion:

> You subjugate the hurricane
> Arising in demented force,
> You hasten back the ocean
> Overflowing on its shores.
>
> You curb the plant in order that
> The giant forest will not hide
> The earth with its destructive shade,
> The grass will not rise to the skies. (134)

In the same way a double significance can be attached to many of
the images in "The Last Death." This symbolic device was
common to much of Baratynsky's early verse, especially that which
used Finnish landscape as background. Here, it receives its ultimate
development, both concretely and abstractly.

This stream of poetic thought eventually touches on mankind,
and just as death curbs the excesses of nature, it reduces human
passions to silence. A generalization typical of the rationalist
manner constitutes the conclusion, which is similar in mood to "Two
Fates." The old opposition of hope and agitation to hopelessness
and peace is expanded to life versus death. The image of the corpses
in the earlier poem contains the seeds of this expansion.

Inseparably coupled with "Death" is "From A. Chénier" (*Iz
A. Shenie*), 1828, written the same year and representing a shortened version of Chénier's "Elégie XXV." This poem falls into
two well-defined parts, each part consisting of one complete sentence. The first corresponds to the ideas of "Death" and reveals

the despondency in which that work was quite possibly written. Emphasizing the close ideological unity is a carry-over of terminology: the "turbulence of existence" and the "hurricane" of "Death" merge into the "storm of the fates," and all three terms subsequently crystallize into the "bondage of existence," with its overtones of necessity. The "peace" (*mir*) of "Death" becomes the "peace" (*pokoy*) of the grave.

The second part, however, effects a turnabout, and no repetitions from the previous poem are apparent. The poet loses his resoluteness and confesses that the thought of the grave is frightful; he had reacted in similar fashion to the sadness of "Truth." It is significant that poetry—the "promises" of the muse— is one of the "pretexts" for living that he offers himself.

The death of Delvig augmented Baratynsky's melancholy. With Delvig went his closest tie with the period of the 1820's, which was coming to represent for him, among other things, the heyday of his poetic popularity. His cheerlessness is expressed in "My Elysium" (*Moy Eliziy*), 1831, in which the future home of the blessed is relocated in the memory of the past.

Indicative of Baratynsky's continuing obsession with death is "A Fragment" (*Otryvok*), 1831, first published under the title "Belief and Unbelief. An Episode from a Poem" (*Vera i neverie. Stsena iz poemy*). Like the preceding lyric, it suggests an acute discontent. What begins as a Romantic contemplation of a pastoral scene evolves into a reasoned dialectic between "Him" and "Her," or "Unbelief" and "Belief." Both presaging and serving as a point of departure for this painful discourse, which is saturated with religious and archaic vocabulary, is his exclamation:

> From these waters, woods and hills
> I lift my gaze up to the skies,
> To the ethereal abode
> And think: the creator is great,
> The world is lovely! . . . (149)

Unable to discern harmony in nature or to be content with its beauty, he lifts his questioning gaze to the heavens, seeking a response he fails to find below. In her subsequent praise of the Creator, however, she asks only that she be spared the grief of outliving her companion, whereupon he becomes visibly distressed:

> Tomorrow...tomorrow...how frightful!
> A corpse unseeing and unhearing,
> A chilly corpse!...The light of day
> Will strike me in the eyes in vain!
> In vain will you cling to my lips,
> With your impassioned lips,
> To me, with overflowing tears,
> With anguished sobbing will you call—
> I'll not awake!...(149)

The image of a dead man, with sightless eyes and stiffened lips, appears suddenly in the green meadow. Similarly had the ancient graves unexpectedly loomed on the table in "Feasts"; in the same manner had Deliya been abruptly reduced to a shriveled hag, and the passionate youths in "Two Fates"—to corpses. These and other contrasts are persistently developed in an entire group of poems. However, at this point Baratynsky goes beyond the extent of his previous thoughts on death: "she" asserts the existence of another life, "Where all the earthly apprehensions/We'll shake away with earthly dust" (150).

The potentiality of a religious solution to inevitable contradictions is treated here for the first time. The possibility of life after death offers hope and peace, as opposed to the "dissonant voices" of this life. He accepts this possibility, but only by dint of the necessity which his unrelenting logic forces upon him; his is primarily a deductive, intellectual decision. After rationalistically setting up five propositions proving the existence of an afterlife, he concludes that "we're in the vale of tribulations/But there's a place of retribution" (151).

This consideration is outlined in the preface to "The Gypsy Girl," where Baratynsky again expresses himself in essentially logical terms: "...this world is the world of tribulations, where for the most part virtue suffers, but vice prospers. From this apparent disorder in the visible world both theologians and philosophers infer the necessity of another life, the necessity of future rewards and punishments, promised us by revelation" (319).

In "A Fragment" this reasoning is approved and God is now justified before the "heart" and the "intellect"—focus of that continual conflict between two mutually exclusive attitudes present in Baratynsky's poetry since its beginnings. Here, a balance, a communication between the two has been established. It is interesting to note, however, that when the poet made the first definitive turn to poetry for consolation in "Stanzas," 1825, he had declared in a similar way that the "gods" were "justified." Like that consolation, which was to be anything but permanent, his vision of an "unsetting day" *(den nezakhodimyy)* in this poem was to be a passing solace. She realizes that his mental exercise has been only an attempt at belief, for she questions the necessity of "persuasions for those persuaded" (151).

A more confident note is struck in "The Madonna" *(Madonna)*, 1832. In this balladlike composition, which attests to Baratynsky's enduring fascination with Italy, it is the Virgin who justifies the unyielding faith placed in her.

One of Baratynsky's few poems to win over-all approval during this period of descent in his popularity was "On the Death of Goethe" *(Na smert Gyote)*, 1832. Commemorating the death of the great German poet, its six stanzas are written in vigorous amphibrachs whose majestic cadence is sustained throughout. The last couplet of each six-line stanza tends to function as a summation, the terseness and conclusiveness of which are emphasized by the finality of the masculine rhyme. Goethe himself is grandly depicted as one who sleeps serenely, certain that he has accomplished every earthly possibility.

This idealized Goethe was one who both responded to and who harmonized the opposing principles within himself, whether they were of the heart or the mind; his "winged thought" circled the world and found a limitation only in the infinite. His immense capabilities receive a constant outward development, so that in the fourth stanza his personality virtually merges with nature in a manner bespeaking the influence of Schelling. In his breadth of comprehension, he encompassed extremes stretching from the seas to the heavens.

In the last two stanzas Goethe is carried to the edge of eternity. However, in these the atmosphere inspired by the teachings of Schelling dissolves, and they reflect Baratynsky's own concern with religion and life beyond the grave. Typically, two reasoned, hypothetical prospects are set forth, the first in stanza five:

> He knew and experienced the whole of man!
>   And if by this temporal lifetime
> The creator limited our fleeting life,
>   And if past the visible world,
> Past death there is nothing more waiting for us—
> His grave will then justify our creator. (157)

The anxiety of "A Fragment" has disappeared, but with it has gone the uncomfortable but undeniable token of affirmation. The notion of vindicating the Creator has been retained, as well as the rationalist procedure which lay at the base of the earlier poem. In the last stanza the other dialectical possibility is expounded with the same impassivity as its opposite:

> If life past the grave is accorded to us,
>   In full having breathed of this life,
> In deep and resounding responses in full
>   All earthly to earth having given,
> With light soul up to the eternal he'll fly,
> In heaven the earthly will not disturb him. (157)

The poet, confronted with an option, declines to choose; in his Hamlet-like vacillation he prefers simply to state the case, elaborating in equal measure on each supposition. He remains suspended in indecisiveness, as he leaves the image of the deceased Goethe suspended between heaven and earth. Whether or not death holds an afterlife is left unresolved, as, in a larger sense, the poet's turn to religion is left undeveloped. Inability to adapt harmoniously to earthly life leads him to look upward, but his visions of eternity prove to be evanescent. Preoccupation with the certainty of death itself is more characteristic for him than consistent construction of a life after death or belief in that life.

IV *Persistence of a Dual Outlook*

Distinctive features of Baratynsky's poetry during the late 1820's and the first half of the 1830's suggest his continued contacts with the Wisdom-lovers. His fascination with certain thematic areas of Schelling's esthetics gave his work a special orientation and tonality which, as noted earlier, tended to blend with its previous inspirations and directions. But the philosopher's higher world of art was at odds with prosaic reality, and recurring oppositions on various levels are persistently manifested in this group of poems during the same period.

"Stanzas" (*Stansy*), 1827, has definite ties with Baratynsky's earlier verse; it is permeated with autobiographical allusions, including his return from Finland and his visit to Mara in the spring of 1827. The mood of serenity brought on by the sight of green hills, a familiar grove, and thickets combines with a quiet reflection on the past from the vantage point of maturity and experience.

Elegiac melancholy is augmented by exceptional euphony, i.e., No *obreló* li *razdelénie*,/No *prinesló* li *plód onó*? ("But did it find participation,/But was a harvest ever reaped?") (133). The "g" (pronounced "k" in final position)—"kh" rhyme (*míg— drugíkh*) in the sixth stanza is reminiscent of eighteenth-century practice, when the Church Slavonic pronunciation of "g" in voiceless position as a fricative was widespread. (Baratynsky uses this rhyme elsewhere; for example, *blág—ottsákh* in the fifth stanza of "The Last Death.")

The same (sixth) stanza with its reference to "brothers," some wandering afar and others no longer alive, is often seen as a direct reference to Kyukhelbeker and other victims of the Decembrist Uprising.[9] The last stanzas recall several of Baratynsky's earliest poems where themes of a "quiet happiness" and a "tender friend" are developed; explicit, as well, is that longing for solitude, poignantly expressed in "Feasts."

Baratynsky's move beyond the strict Classical genre system is apparent in the great majority of all his poems after 1827. Typical, at the same time, is the short lyric known as the anthology poem, whose subject matter was frequently drawn from mythology. This type of lyric, often containing a profound or original thought in concise, elegant form, is exemplified in "We studiously observe the world..." *(Staratelno my nablyudaem svet...)*, 1828. Here the poet is disposed to abandon the strain of all his futile intellectual efforts to unravel the phenomena of existence and to plunge himself into the age-old practicalities of folk wisdom. A like spirit of humility, coupled with the growing reliance on art, penetrates both "My gift is mean and my voice is low..." *(Moy dar ubog, i golos moy ne gromok...)*, 1828, and "The Muse" *(Muza)*, 1829.

The longer and jocular "The Imp" *(Besyonok)*, 1828, is written in folk style and contains elements from Russian songs and tales. Appearing at the wave of a hand, the fabled imp who gently rocked his cradle in childhood revisits the adult to dispel his anguished thought and heal his "sickened spirit." The one, who in an access of depression was ready to throw himself into the wisdom of the folk proverb, now loses himself in the drollery of folk legend. When the shortcomings of reality become intolerable, the imp disperses oppressive thought and simply throws the magic cap *(shapka-nevidimka)* over the globe and it and its troubles disappear.

It offers an escape from discordant reality and becomes a symbol of imagination. And the poet mounts the flying carpet of his fancy, leaving the "dismal truth" behind. The imp thus plays the opposite

role of the "demon" in "When will the darkness disappear...,"
who entraps the spirit and wraps it in a hazy blackness.

In "The Fairy" (Feya), 1829, the poet again retreats to
fantasy, but discovers that he is so tied to the deterministic aspects
of reality that they intrude in his imaginary world. Following the
technique of earlier elegies, he generalizes that "we are slaves"
by virtue of our very spirit. Even the Promethean freedom of the
spirit is fettered to the earth here; the mind, paralyzed by thought,
can see no further than itself. As is much of Baratynsky's verse,
"The Fairy" is symmetrically structured: the first six lines describe
the dream, the second six, the impossibility of happiness in the
dream, and the last six constitute the conclusion.

In two occasional poems of the same year, "To K. A. Sverbeevaya" (K. A. Sverbeevoy) and "To Princess Z. A. Volkonskaya"
(Knyagine Z. A. Volkonskoy), Baratynsky employs the device of
opposition in that particular context which it acquires in poems
such as "The Fairy," "The Imp" and "A wondrous city at times
emerges...," i.e., the juxtaposition of two spheres of vision. As
in the latter poem, for instance, "To K. S. Sverbeevaya" is built on
a simile in reverse order, proceeding from the higher to the lower
realm: a star becomes a woman. In the second lyric, written
on the occasion of Volkonskaya's departure for Italy in early 1829,
the opposition between cold, harsh Russia and "animated,
voluptuous" Italy, in the final analysis, is transformed into one
between death and the "better world" after death.

Opposition of another order is manifest in "Where is the sweet
whisper..." (Gde sladkiy shyopot...), 1831, one of Baratynsky's
few poems in two-foot iambic. In the introductory lines the inert
and sallow profile of winter is set off against the movement and
colors of some earlier spring. A suffocating carpet of grisly whiteness has stifled the landscape and the lively stream has gone silent
beneath its bleak crust of ice. Only the "malicious wind," which
howls and rages, lends motion to a nature suspended in entropy. In
turn the wind grows into a snowstorm; and the poet, cheered by the
play of his fire and separated from the storm by his window, loses
himself in forgetfulness.

Objective description merges with subjectivity in the last stanza,
in which the storm becomes symbolic of inner restlessness and
anarchy. Natural scenery has a similar function in "The Waterfall,"
"The Storm" and "Death," and Baratynsky also links his accounts
of nature with a frame of mind in "Eda" and "The Gypsy Girl."

In this lyric he turns to a "tender love" (155), and attempts to persuade himself that he will forget the "storms of existence" (155) as he forgets the storm outdoors.

The "laws of eternal beauty" have receded from the one gnawed by reflection, and he is not capable of projecting his misery into a celestial framework. He can only invoke Providence and implore self-oblivion, even if it lasts for only a moment, as he has forgotten momentarily the symbol of his troubled reality, the raging storm of nature. His window can protect him from that storm, but not from the one he carries within himself. As that storm devastates the face of nature and leaves in its wake a deathlike stillness, so his own inner convulsions rip him apart. And whereas, in "When will the darkness disappear...," his mental landscape fades into vague blackness, here it becomes a wasteland, terrifying in its whiteness.

"Of what use are the dreams of freedom to a slave?...." (*K chemu nevolniku mechtania svobody?...*), 1833, forms a continuation of the theme of contradictory human experience, subjected to earthly existence. Written in alexandrine couplets, it, unlike "On the Death of Goethe," which reveals a constant outward motion, proceeds on a line which moves twice from an inner to an outer point. This line might be more specifically defined as one which proceeds from the abstract to the concrete, reverts to the abstract, and in its final outward motion, combines both of these directions. This structural design gives "Of what use are the dreams..." ties with certain of Baratynsky's other nature poems, including "The Waterfall" and "Where is the sweet whisper...," both of which, however, are distinguished by concrete-abstract-concrete movement.

The title line formulates the theme, and subsequent lines project this mentality to external points of reference. The deterministic approach in several other poems is given frank expression. The inability of the fir tree to move from its fixed position recalls the inability of the aspen to become the oak in the second epistle to Gnedich,[10] and the prescribed path of the heavenly bodies is a carry-over from the poem dedicated to Sverbeevaya. New in this context are the images of the river, flowing within its banks, and especially the wind, a traditional symbol of freedom,[11] whose motions are prescribed by its own law.

The setting, both mental and material, now ascertained, the theme is developed (return to the abstract). Submission becomes protest. The poet's quiet, resigned peace, achieved through reason, is suddenly converted into agitation. This passage has obvious connections with previous verse; among them, the "slaves" here are immediate counterparts of the "slaves" of necessity in the epistle "To Delvig," whereas the glorification of passions is associated with the second epistle to Yazykov.

The last fragment completes the second return to the concrete, which takes with it the concept of the abstract: "...O burdensome for us/Life, beating in the heart in a mighty wave/And pressed by fate into constricted boundaries" (162). The river noted earlier becomes a submerged symbol, and the concrete delineation of its features elucidates the themes of both submission and rebellion. These are united in the image of the symbolic river, just as they are in the poetic personality. However, nothing is reconciled; the two themes are developed, but not synthesized (as is the purely technical motion of the concrete and the abstract), and continue to exist as separate entities. In the same way the poet in "Finland" contains within himself the two opposites of transience and eternity. In another sense the irresolution reflected in so much of Baratynsky's work is but given another expression.

"Take delight: all passes by!..." (*Naslazhdaytes: vsyo prokhodit!...*), 1834, also has fundamental bonds with the mainstream of Baratynsky's verse. It represents, in particular, a follow-up of an allegorical miniature, "Merriment and Grief" (*Veselie i gore*), 1825, in which the two "disparate friends" are shown to be inseparable partners on the "road of existence." In the present poem moods of derangement and resignation intertwine with Classical fate, which leads capriciously toward both pleasure and misfortune. The second quatrain of the first stanza appears as an echo from "Two Fates," written ten years earlier; but the suppressed emotion that lay concealed behind schematic and logical oppositions has been toned down to unassertive acceptance of discordance. The irony of the title line becomes meek compliance in the second stanza:

> Don't complain: all passes by,
> And to happiness sometimes
> Rigorous adversity
> Brings us unexpectedly.
> And to merriment and sadness
> On this temperamental earth
> In their righteousness the gods
> Have bestowed the self-same wings. (162, 163)

Recurrent terminology heightens the sense of a certain monotony, resulting from unmuffled passivity in regard to the inevitable. At the same time, as in the instance of the mighty river held in abeyance, yet threatening to chaotically overflow its banks at any moment, this quiet statement of resignation in the face of unreconciled, contradictory reality suggests, in its highly controlled restraint and equation of two opposites, a potential of mental collapse.

In formal aspects "Take delight: all passes by!. . . ." displays a balanced progression of four complete sentences, each composed of four lines. The abundance of rhymed "o's" and "a's" conveys an additional impression of uniformity. Use of the Carch Slavonic dual accusative (*krile*—"wings") is indicative of Baratynsky's growing inclination to use archaisms not common to poetry, words which impressed the reader of the time as alien and bizarre.

The lacerating effects of the relentless reflection are also implicit in "Preserve your prudence,. . . ." *Khrani svoyo neopasenie,. . .),* 1834. A young girl is enjoined to transform the world with the whimsicalities of her youthful dreams in order that it remain for her the "quiet paradise" suggested by the flower garden of her school. *Neopasenie* demonstrates another of Baratynsky's tendencies of these years—to alter the meaning of a word by a (usually) negative prefix. Striking examples of others are *nezakhodimyy* ("unsetting") of "A Fragment" and *neobshchiy* ("uncommon") of "The Muse."

"O thought! the flower's fate is yours:. . . ." *(O mysl! tebe udel tsvetka:. . .),* 1834, is preoccupied with the infinitude of the reflective principle. Structured on a comparison which unfolds in a string of graphic, precise imagery, this lyric is again illustrative of Baratynsky's talent for representing a distinctly abstract process in concrete terms. Behind the picture of the blossom besieged by swarming insects, which will, in fading, produce its own seed, arises a concept of mental activity similar in scope and implication. Despite the energy of the procedure, in the very circumstances of its endlessness, it takes on an overtone of immobility. In this paradox is contained the central contradiction of Baratynsky's poetic method; the interminability of his thought, its vitality notwithstanding, incapacitates him, renders him indecisive and stationary.

Closely associated with this feature are his imagery and thematics, conspicuous examples of which are "The Last Death" and "On the Death of Goethe," where the ferment and persistency of speculative thought are climaxed by vast portrayals of motionlessness. On a

smaller scale many of his early and better elegies are part of this
general spectrum.

That he was trapped in this morass and that he longed for escape
and self-forgetfulness are reiterated in "Spring, spring! how pure the
air!..." (*Vesna, vesna! kak vozdukh chist!...*), 1834. A shimmering
description of spring in lively iambs is followed by a Schelling-like
fusion of lyrical subjectivity with nature. The "dissonant feast" of
"A Fragment" is replaced by the blithe "feast" of spring. The one
pursued by thought drinks deeply of oblivion, and in his intoxicat-
tion, flows away with the babbling stream and takes to the air with
the bird.

Infrequently the poet sought retreat, and it is this impulse which
is apparent in "Believe: you, my beloved, are dearer than fame to
me;..." (*O ver: ty, nezhnaya, dorozhe slavy mne;...*), 1834, addressed to his wife. The agitation of the creative experience is too
much and he pleads for respite from the "rebelling muse." In another poem dedicated to Nastasia Lvovna, "A fanciful nickname..."
(*Svoenravnoe prozvanie...*), 1834, tender, lyrical sentiment merges
with a Romanticist notion common to the poetry of Zhukovsky, Lermontov and Tyutchev, among others—that of the "inexpressible."
Language is incapable of expressing the essence of feeling. The
"nickname" (apparently "Popinka"[12]) becomes "...a symbol/Of
feelings whose expression I/Have not found in languages" (168),
and will be the means of recognition amidst the "chasms" of eternity.

The motif of retreat is repeated in "Desolation" (*Zapustenie*),
1834, a description of the park at Mara. Seeking to revive memories
of his childhood and his father, the poet wanders about overgrown
paths, now hardly remembered. Corresponding to the decayed and
deteriorated surroundings is the parallel account of autumn in the
country, with its bare and blackened trees, frostbitten grass, and
atmosphere of fading and decline, all of which is thrown into greater
relief by accompanying digressions on Mara at springtime.

The ending is a tribute to the father, a "friend of reverie and nature," who comprehended the "secret rustling" of the trees. His
shade prophesies a "timeless spring" (*nesrochnaya vesna*) to the
son, in the midst of whose "unfading" (*nevyanushchie*) groves
and "undrying" (*neskudeyushchie*) streams, family ties will be
renewed. Original use of negatives heightens the contrast between
the momentariness of the autumn and the eternity of the spring
which is to come.

It is at once characteristic of Baratynsky that he should insert an image of spring in a description of autumn, that he should plant a dream of freedom in the mind of a slave, juxtapose protest with submission, fantasy with reality. It is apparent, however, that his imagination of hope and escape remained subordinated to the reality of contradiction and tension. As a result he did not succeed in freeing his verse from an over-all atmosphere of elegiac disenchantment and "desolation," interspersed with glimpses of harmony and stability.

o   o   o   o

"Desolation" was one of the last poems that Baratynsky wrote for the 1835 collection; it appeared in April of that year. Unlike the 1827 edition with its genre subdivisions, it consisted of only two parts: Part I was comprised of lyrics, and Part II, of long poems. Of the 131 poems in the first part, seventy-seven had been included in the earlier edition and were grouped mostly in the beginning (many in reworked versions).

The majority of all the poems appeared without titles, as this was in line with Baratynsky's conception of the first part as a continuous and coherent lyrical cycle. With this in mind, he composed (but did not publish) a preface in verse in order to impose additional unity on this poetic biography. He began to prepare the collection as early as 1832, and, once again, he subjected his work to an exacting revision, making it more concise, impersonal, and condensed. Many archaisms, unusual even for poetry written in elevated style, and neologisms bearing an archaic imprint were making their way into his work.

The collection met with a negative reception by the critics and it was greeted with silence by the *Moscow Observer*, the journal that Baratynsky was associated with at the time. He himself thought of it as a completion of his activity as a poet. In 1832 he had written Vyazemsky that "it indeed will be the last and I will add nothing to it."[13] His pessimism in this regard could be directly attributed to a number of factors: the disintegration of his popularity, the death of Delvig, the closing of the *European*—and his own inner difficulties, manifested both in a growing trend toward solitude and isolation, and in the never-ending struggle between two systems of thinking.

If, in the 1827 edition, this struggle had been reflected as a pull between opposites, expressed on a number of levels, then in the

1835 edition, it is made more complex. The struggle itself becomes relegated to a lower world of reality, which is then opposed to a higher place of harmony and synthesis, toward which the poet aspires. The resulting Romantic content continued to be subordinated to an essentially logical and Classical form of expression, indicative of the reflective, intellectual mentality from which it sprang.

In spite of momentary successes, the aspiration as a whole proved to be a failure, and consciousness of failure led to renewed attempts. In this connection his verse was growing narrower in scope and more concentrated. And in the long run he was to remain ensnared between two outlets, and consequently, to become increasingly disillusioned. His last collection, *Twilight*, is a stirring and impressive testament of this disillusionment.

CHAPTER 5

The Poet in Exile

Twilight *(Sumerki)*, connected with the name of a stream,
"Sumer," in the forests surrounding Muranovo,[1] appeared
in 1842. It contains twenty-six poems written during the period
1834 to 1842, many of which are thematically related to one another.

Biographically, this period traced the peak of Baratynsky's
friendship with the Kireevsky circle and, as the latter moved in
the direction of open Slavophilism, its gradual decline. Because
Baratynsky was to assume an ever-decreasing part in the heated
polemics between opposition intellectual groups that began to
dominate Moscow literary life toward the end of the 1830's, he was
considered as little more than a relic of the past, as one unable to
adjust to the new demands and ideas of a new age. As a result he
was subject to an extraordinary sense of frustration and disjunction. Such was the general background against which this collection
and Baratynsky's last poems were written.

I Twilight

The opening epistle, "To Prince Pyotr Andreevich Vyazemsky"
(Knyazyu Petru Andreevichu Vyazemskomu), 1834, sets the tone of
the volume. It also suggests Baratynsky's enduring attachment to
the no-longer popular Arzamas traditions, of which Vyazemsky had
been an outstanding representative. Held together by parallel
syntactic constructions and constant use of obsolete vocabulary,
the epistle purports to be a record of the author's personal experi-
ences. Recapitulated in the first passage are the fundamental thematic features of his poetic trends in their simplest form, including
the "contradictions" and the fascination with Schelling's lofty
conceptions of "beauty" and "good."

The next passage, in which he alludes to himself as a "happy
son of solitude" (172), is perhaps less candid; nor had he really
calmed the conflict between "frivolous dreams of the heart" and

"idle aspirations of thought," still at war within him. An indication of the continued actuality of the struggle is the juxtaposition of two opposites—the "grave" and the "noisy world"—recalling, in particular, "The Skull." Behind the screen of apparent peace, the "Lethe" he had created for himself, the old anxiety and restlessness persist. His seclusion was little more than a defense mechanism, and in the subsequent invocation to Vyazemsky beginning with "O star of pleiad set asunder!" (173) is felt a plea for sympathy and a need for identification with the past.

The oratorical tones of the epistle are resumed in "The Last Poet" (*Posledniy poet*), 1835. Concerned with the degeneration of art in a world absorbed in industrial cares, it reflects the direct influence of the guiding ideology of both the *European* and the *Moscow Observer*. Representative of this ideology was Kireevsky's article, "The Nineteenth Century" (*Devyatnadtsatyy vek*), published in the first number of the *European* in 1832. Kireevsky noted a rise in commercial interests and preoccupations to the detriment of spiritual and artistic values, and surmised that the immediate future presupposed "coldness, prosaism, pragmatism, and, on the whole, an exclusive striving toward practical activity."[2]

The first stanza of Baratynsky's poem, depicting a century marching implacably along its "iron path," voices these sentiments. The "childish dreams of poetry" (173) have disappeared in the general obsession with "the essential" and "the useful." These ideas, together with the opposition of the poet to society, have points of contact with Romanticism, and, for example, can be found in the poetry of Vyazemsky, Pushkin, Delvig, and Lermontov. They represent a further development of earlier themes in Baratynsky's own verse, where the high calling of the poet sets him apart from his environment. In those poems, however, he had been honored, whereas here he is the object of derision. Moreover, as early as 1824, in his epistle to Bogdanovich, Baratynsky had objected to "commercial logic" in connection with poetry.

In contrast to the ponderous iambic pentameter of the first stanza, the second is written in brisk trochaic tetrameter. The change in meter functions to intensify the antithesis of the poet and his countrymen and to make more distinct the difference between his light-minded spontaneity and their serious existence, devoted to progress and science.

Set in contemporary Greece, the "primeval paradise of the muses," the poem acquires an external impression of both history and timeliness. Scientific culture is flourishing, but the melodies of the lyre have died away. The "winter" of a world growing "decrepit" has approached, and mankind is seen as "pale and stern," a picture recalling the physical deterioration of humanity in "The Last Death." In that work humans had been presented as carrying rationalistic and intellectual endeavors to the point of their own destruction, but here the same endeavors have advanced only to the point that poetry can no longer be appreciated.

In contradistinction to decaying winter are the green hills and forests of Parnassus, native land of Homer, where the inspirational spring of Castalia is still flowing forth. It is here that the poet appears as "the unexpected son of the last powers of nature" (174). Poetry is thus paired with nature, and the following stanza represents a further expression of Schelling's teachings and those of his partisans in Russia:

> He, with openheartedness,
> Love and beauty celebrates,
> And of science which defies them
> The conceit and emptiness:
> Transitory sufferings
> Healing with lightmindedness,
> Better, mortal, in ignorant times
> Earth perceives its happiness. (174)

Mankind, in its dedication to science, is cutting its ties with nature and the earth and art, all of which are personified by the poet. This, the central contradiction of the poem, is another reflection of the struggle between opposite attitudes that lay at the basis of most of Baratynsky's previous work. The poet, however, embodies more than poetic imagination and passion. As Yazykov's muse, he comes from a higher realm; and, as in her case, his qualities are exalted in accordance with his origins. He praises love and beauty, the "eternal beauty" of poetry, glorified in the poem, "In days of boundless enthusiasms . . . ;" he brings a new message to a people immersed in utilitarian concerns.

This deprecation of science offended Belinsky deeply,[3] who, taking the words at their face value, essentially failed in his attempt to comprehend the inner division of the one who wrote them. Syntactically, the above passage in the original is illustrative of a tendency becoming more and more evident in Baratynsky's poetry:

conciseness of construction and a corresponding compression of thought at the expense of his former clarity and simplicity.

The poet extols passions, incarnated by Aphrodite, to the worshipers of Urania, the muse of astronomy. His kinship to the goddess of Love and Beauty is emphasized by forms of the same verb (*voznikat*—"appear"), used in connection with the birth of each. And as Aeolus, King of the Winds and viceroy of the gods, brings the pastures to fruitfulness with his "life-giving breath," so it is his mission to instill new life into his people.

The didactic comment of the sixth stanza, which constitutes an appeal in his favor, is given a striking euphony by repetition of verbal and case endings in *im (ym)*:

> I zachém ne predadímsya
> Snám ulýbchivym svoím?
> Zhárkim sérdtsem pokorímsya
> Dúmam khládnym, a ne ím!
> Vérte sládkim ubezhdényam
> Vas laskáyushchikh ochés
> I otrádnym otkrovényam
> Sostradátelnykh nebés! (174)

(And why not release ourselves/To our smiling fantasies?/Why submit with ardent heart/To cold thoughts, and not to them!/Trust the charming inspirations/Of the eyes caressing you/And the soothing revelations/Of the sympathetic skies!)

Characteristic of Baratynsky is the reference in one line to the "ardent heart" followed in the next line by another to "cold thoughts." Characteristic, as well, is the neat symmetrical structure: the two questions of the first quatrain (introduced by one interrogative adverb) are succeeded by the two imperatives of the second quatrain (introduced by one verb). This symmetry is further set off by the rhyming vowels: "i" in the first quatrain and "e" in the second.

The poet, however, is contemptuously rejected by the crowd, embodiment of an unyielding rationality. But the solemnity and oratorical intonation of the language in which his rejection is framed give him added dignity in his apparent disgrace. He seeks seclusion where none is to be found. Somewhat in the manner of the chorus in Athenian drama, the nimble trochees intervene at this point with a comment on the sea. Significant is the thematic linking of Apollo, master musician and god of Light and Truth, with the birthplace of Aphrodite—an age-old symbol of rebellion and anarchy. It is toward the sea that the repudiated poet wanders in desperation.

On a cliff overhanging the sea he sees the ghost of Sappho, the Greek poetess who chose to drown herself rather than live with "rejected love." The import of her appearance is duly acknowledged by the iambs, whose measured progress is interrupted by a spondee in the center of the line: *Siya skala...ten Safo!... golos voln...* (-/-///-/-/) (175). In addition the exclamation is isolated syntactically and thus further emphasized. Rather than submit to the prosaic rationalism of his contemporaries the latter-day disciple of Apollo will respond to the "voice of the waves" and take his "useless gift" with him.

A pronouncement with moralistic overtones by the choruslike commentator concludes the poem, and it is clear that the marching century of the first stanza is actually progressing toward death. And in a deadened world, the sea alone remains a symbol of life. Beside the huge "lifeless skeleton" of the one, ironically silvered and gilded by single-minded humanity, lie the "roaring waters" of the other, adamant in their refusal to be shackled to the splendid, but cold logic of their neighbor. Again Baratynsky juxtaposes two irreconcilable opposites. Moreover, in choosing to drown himself, the poet implicitly chooses life. Accordingly, the poem ends in a paradox, a device perceptible in Baratynsky's work as early as "Finland."

The "last poet" perishes because he is neither understood nor wanted by the public. In the occurrences leading to his destruction he acquires obvious Christ-like qualities. For example, the circumstances of his birth are at once ambiguous and mystical. He is not only the son of nature, but the son of the "last powers" of nature, the implication being that nature is being overcome by wayward mankind, which has forgotten and betrayed her in its "iron" pursuits, and that the poet has come in the interests of her salvation.

He speaks to the worshipers of another deity about the "conceit" and "emptiness" of their concerns; he preaches "blessings." He heals with a "life-giving breath;" he refers to "revelations" and urges his listeners to "believe." His words of prophesy are denied in his homeland. Unlike Christ, however, who isolated Himself for forty days in the wilderness prior to His ministry, the poet seeks isolation only after his mission has failed. On the other hand, like Christ, whose death signified everlasting life, the poet found life, too, in the eternity of the sea, unchanged since the day the sun first arose over its waters.

At the same time the poet is endowed with characteristics of the Greek hierarchy of gods. He was born on the mountain of Parnassus, sacred in Greek mythology, and adjacent to the oracle of Delphi, held to be the center of the world by pilgrims who came in quest of truth. Like Apollo, the poet plays a lyre; and like Apollo, who first taught men the art of healing, he heals. He thus combines within himself separate aspects of both Christian and ancient Greek beliefs. These aspects are integrated in a framework, wherein they function to enhance the distinction between him and the vulgarity of his milieu, and, in the final analysis, they are used as part of the device of opposition.

Written during a period when Baratynsky's own popularity was, for the most part, nonexistent, there can be little doubt that "The Last Poet" is imbued with a certain biographical tonality. Yet what is really relevant here is that he has projected a personal frustration, as well as an inner conflict between opposing principles, onto a universal scale, as he had done many times before in his poetry.

In "The Last Poet" the conflict receives a somewhat different interpretation: what had been presented, broadly speaking, as a collision between mutually exclusive attitudes, and subsequently, as a collision between reality and a higher world of poetry, now takes the form of a clash between poetry and practicality, esthetics and materialism. Being an outgrowth of the basic ideas of his previous work and retaining close connections with that work, this new content was essentially no more than another statement of a reflective mind, forever absorbed in a struggle between opposites. And while it is perhaps true that Baratynsky, like Tyutchev, for instance, did see something profoundly prosaic in the bourgeois world,[4] this outlook was reflected only incidentally in "The Last Poet." It provided but another context for the expression of an internal dialectic that had been inherent in his poetry since its beginnings.

"The Last Poet" also represents a continuation of Baratynsky's predilection for Classically symmetrical form. It unfolds in deductive fashion, showing a logical progression from the general to the particular. Lending a sense of balance and uniformity is the equal number (five) of iambic and trochaic stanzas, each composed of eight lines and each succeeding the other in unfailing sequence.

The device of opposition is a constant throughout. Included here, as in the case of "The Last Death," is the contradiction between the harmony and logic on the technical level and the implicit rejection of reason on the thematic level.

The first line of thought presented in "The Last Poet," namely that of the "iron age," penetrates "Prejudice! it is a fragment..." (*Predrassudok! on oblomok...*) 1841. An allegory of prejudice in terse, condensed phraseology, it depicts the "haughty century" racing along, unable in its blindness to distinguish truth from its own prejudice. Complementing it is the next lyric in *Twilight*, "Novinskoe," 1841, a miniature dedicated to Pushkin, which is concerned with the "subtle dream" of poetic inspiration.

The same dichotomy is developed even more fundamentally in "Signs" (*Primety*), 1839. The first five stanzas portray the close relationship of nature and primitive man, who loved and trusted in childlike fashion the wild forests surrounding him. In return, he was protected by nature, who, for instance, cautioned him through the raven when danger was near and foretold victory over an enemy through the wolf. The corollary is drawn in the last stanza, where modern man, trusting in "intellect" rather than in intuitive "feeling," has thereby alienated himself from nature.

Feeling and passion are glorified in a different perspective in "Always in both purple and in gold,..." (*Vsegda i v purpure i v zlate,...*), 1840, which contains the ultimate paradox and irony: the one whose "undimming passions" are being praised is a ghost.

Perhaps one of Baratynsky's supreme achievements in the positing of irreconcilable opposites is "The Stillborn" (*Nedonosok*), 1835, a poem which has direct connections with the main body of all his work. It is here that he embodies and symbolizes both the final indecisiveness of a poetic outlook trapped between extremes and the inconsolable disillusionment and sense of tragedy resulting from that untenable position.

The first stanza presents the leading image in this soliloquy of impotence and self-contempt and may be seen as the sequel to the epistle "To Delvig," written some fourteen years earlier. The "comforting death" spoken of in the epistle has proved to be illusory. The "illness of life," bearable because it was temporary, has been carried over into eternity. The "blind slave," deprived of apparent dignity and worth in death, has been reduced to a weak and insignificant half-soul, a neuter, condemned to hover forever "between heaven and earth" (178).

Eternity is infinitely worse than life; the one who figuratively flew round "the steppes of the world" in anguish ("To Prince Pyotr Andreevich Vyazemsky") as a mortal, now will do so perpetually as a "winged sigh." This emasculated apparition, which can hardly fly up to the clouds without falling downward, is the antithesis of Goethe's spirit, pictured as flying up to meet eternity with strength and self-assurance. The discrepancy between the measured and stately amphibrachs of that poem, and the jerky and mangled impression given by the trochees in this case heightens the contrast.

Denied access to the paradise beyond the clouds, it is nevertheless allowed to "play" in the vicinity during good weather. In this quasi-idyllic account the repeated references to wings assume a logical expansion to a bird; but its lightsome trills, the first indication of sound in a thus-far silent tableau, are brusquely hushed by the booming of a storm. The bright dome of heaven is suddenly darkened, and in the pandemonium which ensues, the tiny spirit is shunted and tossed about by the elements. No longer a bird, fawning before the rays of the sun—again, a pointed contrast to Goethe's eagle—it resembles now merely the "down" of a bird and is on a par with the dust of the earth.

The dissonance and roar of the storm are intensified by the following onomatopoetic passage:

> Búri grókhot, búri svíst!
> Víkhor khládnyy! Víkhor zhgúchiy!
> Byót menyá drevésnyy líst,
> Udusháet prákh letúchiy! (178)

Out of this turmoil emerges the image of a violent whirlwind, with its extremes of heat and cold; again the little apparition is caught between absolutes. Staccato rhythm and syntactic inversion assist in conveying the topsy-turvy, anarchical character of the storm.

The "earthly dust" shaken off by the dead in "A Fragment" chokes and suffocates in this vision of eternity. Subsequently, the despondent wail of the "stillborn" is lost in the jarring discords of heaven and earth, as the noise and uproar of nature's storm blend into the storm and confusion of human existence: wars, passions, the cry of a sickly infant. In heaven the once-exalted "gardens of poetry" ("In days of boundless enthusiasms . . .") have been replaced by the empty immensity of barren "fields." This terrifying infinity would have been viewed in another way by Goethe,

who "found a limit only in limitlessness." But the misfit
spirit, alienated equally from heaven and earth, and tearing about
between the two, can only seek to "muffle" the sounds of one
storm with those of another.

The concluding stanza appears as the resolution to the first and
gives substance and specification to the "winged sigh":

> As in haze I see the world;
> Echo of celestial harps
> I hear faintly. . . On the earth
> I incarnated a stillborn.
> It took leave without existence:
> Fatal temporality!
> Your resplendence is a burden,
> Meaningless eternity! (179)

The morbid form at last confesses that it is the soul of an aborted
baby, who existed for its assigned time on earth "without existence." Its ephemerality in the world is opposed to the eternity of
its spirit in a typically Romantic division of the body and soul; but
as "fatal temporality" carries a hint of parody on Romanticism,
this version of immortality appears as a distortion of the Romanticist conceptions of the afterlife as a whole.

The "stillborn" combines qualities of its predecessors, the "imp"
and the "demon." As these, it symbolizes an abstract frame of
mind in concrete terms. Moreover, it synthesizes the higher
realm of the one and the lower realm of the other. But this is a
sterile synthesis, lacking a higher stage of truth and indicating but
an immobile suspension between thesis and antithesis. The world,
seen through haze, is as far away as the heavenly harps. The flash
of life on earth is deprived of significance; it is being without being.
This contradiction recalls the "last poet," whose life, in the final
analysis, is robbed of meaning as well. Neither is equipped to cope
with life on its own terms, and both perish.

But if the poet finds life and meaning in death, the "stillborn"
discovers that its eternity has no meaning and is but a resumption
of the conditions of life. In this connection it may be seen how
Baratynsky has expanded an inner conflict between two uncompromising principles to a treatise dealing with the paradoxical
foundations of human nature. Man, by his disposition, is necessarily
bifurcated: bound to the earth by his body, his spirit attempts to
overcome this confinement by penetrating to the paradise shimmer-

ing through the clouds. Because of his dual origins he is refused entry, and he remains Romantically displaced and lost on the road between his two native spheres; he belongs nowhere. And by the process of logical extension, Baratynsky proceeds to create an anti-eternity, which has all the contradictory features of earthly existence.

The image of a stillborn child, Naturalistic in its repellency, stands as a symbol of this basic internal conflict and of poetic thought, struggling in vain to free itself from ambiguity. Accordingly, all of the major images in "The Stillborn" acquire a double significance; beyond the sensual level can be perceived the flight of this thought in all its power and impotence.

More Classical in aspect are the three following anthology poems in *Twilight,* which are written in elegiac distichs. "Alcibiades" *(Alkiviad),* 1835, depicts the young Alcibiades surrounded by a jeering throng to which he is oblivious. Unlike "The Last Poet," reassurance of an ultimate fame is offered to one scorned by his peers. This opposition between an uncomprehending crowd and an individual awaiting a future glory is succeeded in "The Complaint" *(Ropot),* 1841, by juxtaposition of "powerfully-winged thought" and a "kiss of ardent love." Addressed to a bothersome fly which poisons a beautiful summer, it contains two subsequent contradictions: "You of a dreamer reposeful, child of European enchantments/Barbarous Scythian make, enemy avid of death." (180).

The poet, by combining in his nature traits both of the reflective "European" and the savage "Scythian," again has invested a personal conflict with universal proportions having far-reaching implications. This particular dichotomy was to become a major theme in later Russian literature, receiving perhaps its highest expressions in the poetry of Alexander Blok and the Symbolist novel *Petersburg* of Andrey Bely.

The beginning of "To the Wise Man" *(Mudretsu),* 1840, is outwardly reminiscent of "Two Fates" with its postulation of uncompromising opposites. Whereas in the earlier poem, however, "hope and agitation" were opposed to "hopelessness and peace," this antipathy is reflected here in the single concept of "turbulent life," which is then contrasted to "cold death." The opposition is thus between the agitation of life and the inactivity of death. In a series of poems written at the end of the 1820's and the beginning of the 1830's, Baratynsky had associated the discordance of thought with a lower realm, to which he opposed a higher place of harmony.

In the present context the dialectic continues, but unrelieved despair is noted in the replacement of the higher harmony with the harmony and peace of death.

At the same time agitation and dissension are given a new, philosophical interpretation: inner disturbance is a necessary feature of human temperament, in general, and of the artistic temperament, in particular. Peace is impossible and unrest, as the "law of the world," apprehended even by the infant, is unavoidable. The consequence of the theory, that "the troubled word of creative work" raises men from insignificance and sets them apart, is common to Romantic poetry and is understood in "The Last Poet," as well as in others.

The incongruity between youth and age is shown in "Filida, with each winter, . . ." *(Filida s kazhdoyu zimoyu, . . .)*, 1838, an epigram, which characterizes an aging woman who is partial to youthful décolletage. The jocular intonation of the first stanza is expanded to a grim symbolism in the second, which is accompanied by an increase in archaic vocabulary, contributing to its solemnity. Filida reappears as the goddess Aphrodite, suddenly grown old and approaching her death bed instead of the "couch of sleep." The same technique of extension is employed in another epigram of the same year, "Alas! Secondary writer!..." *(Uvy! Tvorets ne pervykh sil!...)*.

The more lyrical "The Goblet" *(Bokal)*, 1835, evokes in reverse many of Baratynsky's early poetic praises of the bottle and its delights. Gone now are the "wide goblets" mentioned in the first part of "Feasts," which poured "merriment into the heart"; gone, as well, are the "full cups" of epicurean oblivion, lauded in the "Epistle to B[aron] Delvig." Naiveté and revelry have been supplanted by a seasoned preference for inspirational solitude, which loosens the flow of thought and liberates repressed dreams. That this silent "orgy" is largely a defense mechanism is indicated by the accumulation of negatives in the third stanza. The same rupture that stood between the "last poet" and his contemporaries, that is, their inability to comprehend and appreciate him, is reiterated with poignant despondency.

Moreover, the youth who in "Feasts" exclaimed in an excess of enthusiasm and mock solemnity: "O kindly Kom, god of the table/ In your delights there is no poison!" (222), now craves "ecstasies" and the "poisons of existence" in equal measure. His invocation to the "goblet of solitude" records the inner changes he has undergone. In substituting this goblet for the fraternal loving cup, he

stands above the inflated mediocrity that surrounds him and is privy
both to the "revelations of Hades" (182) and "celestial dreams."
This theme receives a further development in the last stanza:

> And alone I drink henceforward!
> Not in human noise the prophet—
> But in silent, barren lands
> Finds an elevated realm.
> Not in unavailing pleasure
> Of communal ecstasies—
> But in solitary rapture
> From his eyes the haze will fall! (182)

The opposition between the poet and his milieu is continued.
And in his solitude he attains the status of a "prophet," who lives
in another world. Again, obsolete terminology accentuates his elevated role. However, the outlines of his lofty world are perhaps de-
liberately left vague, and they appear only as a vestige of the "poetic" world of the past. The attempt to escape, to make of his seclusion
a positive phenomenon, is unconvincing and leaves the impression
that constant discord between two poles of thought, between dreams
of heaven and revelations of hell, has been complicated by an un-
wanted and unbearable sense of isolation.

That discord is intertwined with another factor—that of advancing
age—in "There were storms, inclement times,..." (*Byli buri, nepo-
gody,...*), 1839. The first three couplets deal with the youth and his
release from dejection through poetry, and as in "Where is the sweet
whisper...," images of weather take on a twofold significance, reflecting a frame of mind beyond their literal denotation. The last
three couplets depict the older man. To the "black thought" that
was a burden in youth is now added a second burden: "white hair."
And just as black is the antithesis of white and there can be no logical compromise between perpetual opposites, so is it impossible to
harmonize enduring disillusionment with old age. This "double
burden" is too heavy for one who is already tired. The aphoristic
clarity of the final couplet contains no hopes or prospects.

The same atmosphere of futility and despair pervades "Of what
use are you, days!..." (*Na chto vy, dni!...*), 1840. The theme of a
soul which has sustained the ultimate in experience and can be disturbed no more appeared in Baratynsky's earliest elegies, but the
then-vacillating disappointment is now given a point-blank and
finalized statement. The process of "disenchantment" that had not

yet been completed in "Truth" has run its course at last, and the tumult and frenzy of the past have been stilled; the future can offer only "repetitions."

The soul drowses, by now having closed the "narrow circle of sublunar impressions." Its gentle sleep transforms the endless recurrence of day and night, of phenomena already familiar to it, into a subdued, untroubled dream. The body, home of the reposing soul, is left to gaze senselessly as the light of morning slowly vanishes without a trace in the darkness of night: the "barren evening" is ironically "the crown of the empty day!" (183).

As eternity was meaningless in "The Stillborn," it is earthly life which becomes meaningless here. As the soul was suspended between heaven and earth in that context, here it lies paralyzed in a void, which is rippled only by the vague, never-ending motion of the sun. Unlike the division of body and soul which occurs when the body dies, while the body lives, the soul must continue to inhabit it, no matter what the discrepancy in development between the one and the other. The soul is thus imprisoned in the body and maintains an anachronistic relationship with it.

Centering the attention on this mutual incompatibility is the single use of the nouns "soul" and "body"; in other instances pronouns are employed, and "it" (*ono*), situated at the end of the third stanza, with its antecedent in "body" (*telo*—third line, second stanza), acts to throw the body into greater psychological relief by its position both in the rhyme and the enjambment.[5] Adding to the spectral effect produced by the body is the submerged image of the eyes (in the verb *glyadet*—to gaze"). "It" looks on insensibly at the timeless and needless succession of the pallor of day and the blackness of night—the only evidence of color in an otherwise toneless and silent world.

"Achilles" (*Akhill*), 1841, offers the possibility of a release from this limbo; it also continues the religious orientation of "A Fragment." Structured on the familiar extended parallel, its first stanza depicts Achilles, mighty in battle and vulnerable only in his heel. The second is concerned with the modern "warrior": the physical strength of Achilles has been transferred to a spiritual plane, just as his earthly battle has assumed the form of a "higher struggle." Unlike Achilles, who was dipped in the River Styx and made invulnerable everywhere except in the heel, the fighter of today, washed in the font of suffering, is open to attack everywhere except in the heel.

The figure of Achilles thus serves as the point of departure for a meditation which becomes metaphysical in scope. Concrete imagery is projected into a realm of abstract thought processes. At the same time the projection, in the case of the heel, results in embodiment of opposite qualities. A symbol of weakness, it becomes in its abstract frame of reference a symbol of strength. It is the notion of strength which unifies the poem organically. The religious vocabulary creates an appropriate atmosphere for the "living faith" of the conclusion—a resolution which remains conditional and undeveloped. The struggle itself is left in clearer focus.

"At first the thought, embodied in . . ." (*Snachala mysl, voploshchena...*), 1837, is built on a series of extended similes. Recalling "O thought! the flower's fate is yours: . . ." it portrays the degeneration of thought rather than its interminability. A thought is traced from its consecutive appearances, first in a poem (where it is vague, "like a young maiden"), then in a novel (evasive and talkative, "like an experienced wife"), and finally, in journalistic polemics where it engenders only that which is "already known by everybody" (like an "old chatterbox"). Reflecting, perhaps, the author's dissatisfaction with the rise of prose at the expense of poetry[6]—a trend which was instrumental in bringing about his own lack of an audience—the poem echoes the leading idea of "The Last Poet" and "The Goblet."

Similar to "Preserve your prudence, . . ." in intonation and texture is "I'm not yet ancient as a patriarch; . . ." (*Eschyo, kak patriarkh, ne dreven ya; . . .*), 1839. Youth is again contrasted with age, and the picture of an elderly man giving the blessing of youth to a girl is compared with the solemn benediction of a patriarch. Noted here, as in many of the works in *Twilight*, is Baratynsky's tendency to juxtapose archaic and prosaic terminology: the colloquial use of the attributive *drevniy* ("ancient"), followed by the elevated *glava* ("head").

"Disquieting day is pleasant to the crowd, . . ." (*Tolpe trevozhnyy den priveten, . . .*), 1839, sets the poet apart from the public, a polarity that becomes a leitmotif in *Twilight*. It is framed here in one of Tyutchev's favorite oppositions, that of night and day. The "crowd" prefers the friendliness of the troubled day to the horror of the speechless night. The rationality of this preference is apparent in the fear of "unfettered dream of capricious visions" (185) unleashed by the darkness. The night, however, is a source of inspiration to the poet and its "light-winged fantasies" proffer an escape from the "visions" of day—"human vanities, earthly cares" (185).

In the second part the poet seeks to enlighten and to initiate in language penetrated with psychological epithets and synesthetic perceptions. For example, personified "horror" smiles, and the resulting incongruity blends conceptions both concrete and abstract. Striking expressiveness is continued in the last part, which consists of an exhortation the poet addresses to himself. As he had lectured to others on the night, he now gives himself counsel on the daylight.

If "The Stillborn" lends itself to the interpretation of the poet as an exile, in this poem he is the "happy favorite of beneficent fairies," the "cheerful family man, the usual guest at the feast/ Of intangible powers" (185)—another externalization and objective embodiment of something purely subjective in nature. Behind the originality of these semantic combinations stood, in part, the tradition of both Derzhavin and Lermontov.[7] Just as when darkness was "felt," its frightening apparition would disappear, so it is with the "cloud" of "earthly care" thrown over the day. Once it is "touched," it too will disappear and "the gates of the dwellings of the spirits will open" (186) once more.

Commonplace, troubled reality is transformed by poetic imagination and fantasy, and the visionary world thus created is preferred to that reality. In striving to accommodate himself to the day, the poet at once endeavors both to deny its existence and to superimpose on it his own ideals made manifest by the night. Such an endeavor has clear connections with Baratynsky's work of the late 1820's and early 1830's, yet there is a qualitative distinction. A lower world of discord had been contrasted in that work to a higher world of poetic harmony. Here a discordant actuality is juxtaposed with a realm of fantasy. This carefree realm, however, is situated not in the heavens, but in the depths of night; and the poet is not a god on earth, but a "child" of darkness. Whereas he is still involved in the secret, magical process of poetic creativity, there are no "laws of eternal beauty" or "gardens of sacred poetry" before him. No longer "honored by earthly peoples," he is alone at his symbolic "feast," in the same way as he was alone with his bottle in "The Goblet."

The two following lyrics in *Twilight* also evince a concern for poetry. The first, "Hail, sweet-voiced youth!...." *(Zdravstvuy, otrok sladkoglasnyy!...)*, 1841, is addressed to a young poet who is only beginning his "happy" and "glorious" career. The second, "What kind of rhymes?..." *(Chto za zvuki?...)*, 1841, is addressed to an old man whose poetic activity is nearing its end. Destitute and blind he is surrounded by a jeering rabble, resembling a "pack of malicious dogs" in its ferocity.

Nevertheless he is unable to repudiate his long-standing alliance with the muse and understands that art is older than artists, that it will survive the times when its disciples are ridiculed by an uncomprehending public. In the closing stanza earthly glory is postponed to the future, when perhaps his prophetic voice will resound above, "there," "in the celestial priesthood."

"Thought, thought alone!..." (*Vsyo mysl da mysl!...*), 1840, is yet another statement on art and the "artist of the word," in particular. Connected in general aspects with the main currents of Baratynsky's verse, it represents a direct follow-up to the dictum of "To the Wise Man" that "life and agitation are one." The one who drank "oblivion" of thought at the feast of spring in "Spring, spring! how pure the air!..." now realizes that any kind of permanent "oblivion" is not to be his. Moreover, the compulsion to think, to reflect endlessly on the contradictions of phenomena and existence, and, as a result, to become irretrievably enmeshed in those contradictions, has overcome the imaginative faculties which held the possibility of escape from the ensuing intellectual morass.

Thought has stripped everything of romance, of enchantment, of the faintest trace of idealism—"man, and the world,/And death and life...." Truth lies exposed, "without cover," just as the ultimate fate of the world was inexorably shorn of its last "cover" in "The Last Death." It is dissected constantly by relentless analysis; the repetition of "and" transmits the impression of persistency. The "priest" of thought thus becomes its victim—still another contradiction, supremely ironic in its conclusiveness.

Whereas in "To the Wise Man," inner disturbance had been linked to the artistic disposition, here a line is drawn between the literary artist and his counterparts. The "sensual" character of sculpture, music, and painting, as compared with the logical, abstract nature of the word is accentuated by the heavy spondee occurring in the middle of the line: *Rezets, organ, kist! schastliv, kto vlekom* (-/-///-/-/) (187). Those involved in the sensual arts are spared the stifling mental activity inevitably associated with the word and can indulge themselves at life's "holiday." On the other hand, the artist of the word has no respite and the "sharp beam" of thought is forever before him; the static features of his dilemma are fixed by the infrequency of verbs.

The restless dialectic that was set in motion in the naïve epistle to Krenitsyn, written twenty-one years earlier, with its guileless, but painful opposition of antithetic attitudes, proved to be the beginning of an unending, self-defeating process, which was to find no permanent solution. Moreover, the energy of thought, formerly directed toward extraneous objects, searches for a point of reference here, and finding none, it turns its penetrating focus upon itself. What results is a deadening perplexity—creation of a rationalist procedure carried to its logical extreme. Wishing to escape from this work of his own mind, the poet stands helpless and transfixed, as before a "bared sword," which takes from living all its spontaneity and pleasure.

In "The Sculptor" *(Skulptor)*, 1841, Baratynsky returns to the sensual arts. A retelling of the story of Pygmalion and Galatea, it depicts the passionate sculptor gazing at the stone, as each "insinuating caress" of his chisel chips away the covering which conceals the hidden goddess. His truth, embodied in the long-desired Galatea, appears after he has removed the "last cover" from her emerging figure—a decisive contrast to the abstract truth "without cover" of the previous poem. The conclusion represents another example of Baratynsky's difficult syntactic construction, with its sentence extended over two stanzas and insertion of complete subordinate clauses between the main verb and object.

One of the greatest achievements of *Twilight* and of Baratynsky's entire poetic output is "Autumn" *(Osen)*, 1836-1837. Composed of sixteen ten-line stanzas, each of which observes a consistent pattern of rhyme, it is written in a Classically oratorical manner, making maximum use of elevated and archaic terminology. Supporting the eloquence and solemnity are the ponderous five and four-foot iambs, which move grandly and flawlessly from beginning to end.

The first three stanzas, constituting the quintessence of Baratynsky's nature poetry, are a picture of autumn in the country. The first depicts the stillness at the close of summer and recalls autumnal scenes in "Desolation." Rippling waters reflect the "uncertain gold" of the sun's rays, the hills are shrouded in a grey mist, the valleys are submerged in dew. The lively birds have fallen silent, the woods are mute, and the skies are soundless. Nature thus awaits quietly the onslaught of winter. At variance with its apprehensive hush are its brilliant colors, a variance emphasized by the frequent positioning of predicate adjectives and verbs of color and silence in front of their respective nouns.

The next stanza shows the slow but inevitable march of autumn. Lending movement to the landscape and stressing the changes it will undergo is the accumulation of strategically placed verbs. If color and noiselessness were accentuated in the first stanza, it is motion which is in focus here. The finality of the "evening of the year" is marked by the enjambment ("And here's September! and evening of the year / Approaches...)" (188). Many of the images of the beginning stanza reappear: the hills and fields are covered with frost; the forest, no longer speechless, will wail as its leaves are torn away to cover the valley; and the murky river will reflect the darkened sky.

In the third stanza, begun with a farewell to summer both lyrical and oratorical, winter itself is near:

> Farewell, farewell, resplendence of the skies!
>   Farewell, farewell, delights of nature!
> The forest is filled with bewitching whispers,
>   And golden-scaly are the waters!
> The cheerful dream of passing summer joys!
>   An echo in the naked groves
> A woodcutter harasses with an ax,
>   And presently the wintry sight
> Of its oak groves and hills whitened with snow
> The frozen stream will mistily reflect. (189)

Frequently recurring throughout are the rhythmic-syntactical parallelisms exemplified in the first two lines. Characteristic of Baratynsky's verse during his later periods is the use of neologisms, many of which are formed from obsolete elements, as, for instance, is *zlatocheshuychatyy* ("golden-scaly"), a term combining sensations of sight and touch. Another conspicuous instance of his twisted syntax (in the original) is the last three lines above, where the main clause is preceded by its direct object, which, in turn, is preceded by two sets of its own modifiers.

Soon the stream will freeze and the bare trees and hills will be wrapped in snow. The inactivity of winter is further suggested by the small number of verbs. The bliss of summer becomes a dream, disturbed by the ax of a woodcutter—reminder of the impending cold. His appearance provides an easy transition to the following detailed description of harvest time.

The peasant begins to gather the fruit of his labors: after mowing the grass of the valleys and sweeping it into ricks, he hurries to the fields. Sheaves of grain are stacked into luminescent shocks or carried to the village, where a "golden-roofed city" arises around the huts. There the threshing begins and the millstones start to turn.

He has reaped a plentiful yield from his crops, which will sustain him during the coming winter.

Stanza six sets forth the negative member of the parallel upon which "Autumn" is structured: the lyrical personality, begetter of thoughts and faced with spiritual impoverishment, as opposed to the peasant, producer of material goods and rewarded with an abundant harvest. A shift is thus made from a physical, objective level to a speculative, abstract level. Accompanying the shift is a carry-over of the terminology used in connection with the autumn harvest of the peasant, a device which imposes thematic and formal unity. This concrete terminology is now transposed to a metaphysical plane, and the landscape becomes symbolic of a frame of mind. The concept of autumn, as well, is expanded to embrace the "autumn" of the soul, of life in its entirety, a time of fading and disintegration and death.

The tranquil, balanced painting of nature and the fields is abruptly replaced by an uneasy and disturbed intonation, almost psychotic in its bitterness and irony. This change is signaled at the beginning of the stanza by "But you,...," which indicates both contrast and the introduction of a personal inflection. The "plowman of life's field" also looks forward to "harvest" time, when his "furrows" will recompense his "labor of existence." He garners the fruit produced by his "seeds of thought," a motif foreshadowed in "O thought! the flower's fate is yours:...." The analogies with the peasant continue to unfold with stubborn and desperate logic. The constant repetition of the personal pronoun "you" (*ty*) punctuates the introspective character of the monologue and points up the similarities in the comparison: the one, as the other, sowed seeds with hope; both awaited a day of reward.

That day has arrived, but unlike the peasant, the sower of thoughts greets it with an outburst of impassioned and sardonic acerbity. All his work has been useless, and instead of a rich harvest, it brings only a sense of impotent frustration and deep offense. "Dreams" and "passions"—all his "worldly labors"—are discredited. The day of reckoning has come, but it is hollow and fruitless, as it has not brought with it any hint of resolution to the thoughts that he has nurtured within himself for so long. He despises both his youthful fantasies and his intellect; nevertheless, as in "Thought, thought alone!...," he is unable to escape his persistent trend of reflection, and he continues to lay himself bare, stripping his despair of every trace of illusion:

You, at one time the friend of all diversions,
   The ardent seeker of affections,
The tsar of grand obscurities—and now
   The spectator of barren thickets,
Alone with grief, of which the mortal groan
Is hardly stifled by your arrogance. (190)

The contrast with the past, reminiscent of many of Baratynsky's first elegies and epistles, underlines the misery of the present. And the soul, far from being insensitive, as it was in "Of what use are you, days!...," where it drowsed between an "empty day" and a "barren evening," takes active affront. The "mighty wave" of the river in "Of what use are the dreams of freedom to a slave?...." has as if overflowed its banks, and, in so doing, it creates an inner delirium. Thought is suffused with feeling, but no suggestion of balance is perceptible. The poet reaches a stage of mental destitution, and his thought struggles to convey the rational, while in fact it is overcome by passion. Preserving the external aspects of logic, it expresses feverish emotion. His "barren thickets" are the antithesis to a fruitful harvest, and in an outrage of disillusionment, his anguish battles with his pride.

Smothering a groan of indignation that longs to escape from the depths of his being, he holds to his course; and imposing outward order on internal anarchy, he pursues the parallel with the peasant and proceeds to throw a harvest celebration. The "generous host" seats his guests at a table shining with abstract "edibles," just as he himself attended a "feast of intangible powers" in "Disquieting day is pleasant to the crowd,...." However, the diversity of dainties that he serves here all have the same bitter taste, the feast turns into a funeral supper, and in the end he mourns in solitude the departure of "earthly joys."

In "Truth" the poet had cringed before the "truth" of reason, seeing in it only a grave for "earthly joys." And having rejected reason and thus renewed the possibility for resurrection of his joys, he has retained the analytical method of a reasoning mind, which has, in turn, destroyed anew that possibility. Accordingly, he finds himself again in the grave into which he had lowered himself in "When will the darkness disappear..." and choked by the same sepulchral embankment of thought as before.

From this vantage point he contemplates two options open to him: the first of these is to seek once more the guidance of his earlier "truth." In stanza eleven, in a concentrated mixture of prosaic and archaic terminology and involved syntactical inversions, this outlet is explored. "Thoughts" and "feelings"—the old collision—have combined, but not merged. Rather, they are thrown together in a gyrating whirlwind, awaiting resolution. Moreover, the appeal to the intellect to "soothe the trembling of the heart" is deprecated by the attributive "useless."

Instead of accepting the "gift of experience" and its corollary, a "numbing cold," another release is conceivable—religion. This motif is elucidated in a sentence (actually, an independent clause) which includes the whole of the twelfth and thirteenth stanzas. Held together basically by three gerunds (*otryakhnuv*—"having shaken off," *zavidya*—"discerning," *doveryas*—"trusting in"), a present active particple (*vnimayushchiy*—"listening") and a perfective verb in the future (*padyosh*—"fall"), all of which modify an imperative (*znay*—"know")—which itself is directly connected with the beginning of stanza eleven—these two stanzas apply the grammatical principle of subordination to the detriment of clarity. Reflected in this immense sentence, with its throng of dependent clauses, is the reasoning mentality, which makes full use of hypothesis and deductive logic:

> Or, having shaken off the ghosts of earth
>> In an impulse of quickening sorrow,
> Discerning its frontier not far away,
>> The flowering shore beyond black mist,
> The land of retributions, trusting in
>> The dreams proclaimed with strengthened feeling,
> And to the restless voices of this life,
>> United in one glorious hymn,
> Now listening, as to harps, whose harmony
> Magnificent was not perceived by you,—
>
> Before a providence now justified
>> With grateful meekness will you fall,
> With hopefulness that sees no boundaries,
>> And with quieted understanding,—
> Know, that your inner self you never will
>> Communicate to earthly sound
> And to complaisant sons of temporal cares
>> You'll not impart your realization;
> Know, heavenly or of the world, that it
> Was given us on earth but not for earth. (191,192)

Religion as a possible avenue of retreat stretches as far back as "A Fragment," and the idea of a "justified" Providence is directly reminiscent of that poem as well as of certain others. The "flowering shore beyond black mist" holds out recompense for labor unrewarded on earth. Its lofty array of harps, of whose melodies the "stillborn" could hear only an echo, extends harmony and reconciliation to the "restless voices of existence."

But in accepting either of these alternatives, the earthly or the celestial, the intellect or religion, the poet will be denied complete gratification. At this point a theme unfolds which was prefigured in "A fanciful nickname . . ." and the elements of which appeared in Baratynsky's poetry as early as 1821 in the Anacreontic lyric, "To Lida," namely, that of the inexpressible. Here it is laid out in profound and expanded terms, so that it embraces an entire emotional and philosophical complex of attitudes.

The impossibility of expressing the inmost being in the form of "earthly sound" automatically deprives existence of any ultimate, complete sense of fulfillment. The use of the word *vnutrennyaya* ("inner" self) in this connection represents an original use of a feminine adjective as a noun.[8] Such a theme, essentially Romantic, was developed by other Russian poets in various contexts, notably by Tyutchev in the poem "Silentium."[9]

The concept of "earthly sound" is elaborated upon in the fourteenth stanza, which is structured on a simile in reverse order, the figurative preceding the literal. The hurricane convulses the earth, just as the voice of a conceited, commonplace "prophet" draws a reaction from a crowd submerged in lethargic slumber. On the other hand, that voice which has transcended the worldly, which has stepped over the boundary dividing the lower from the higher, finds no response on the earth.

As the hurricane evokes a response only within its own domain—the earth, the disappearance of a star and subsequent appearance of another (stanza fifteen) are of exclusive concern to the heavens. The earthly and the heavenly represent two separate and mutually isolated spheres, and neither answers to the other. Only the poet, who carries within himself an essence "given us on earth but not for earth" is a point of contact between the two worlds. This notion was especially liked by the Symbolists. Affirmed by Derzhavin, but in another context,[10] the idea is also to be inferred from such of Baratynsky's poems as "To Delvig," "The Last Poet," and "The Stillborn." He saw in it a manifestation of mankind's paradoxical makeup, a source both of his highest worth and greatest frustration.

This irresolvable contradiction is superimposed on the opposition between the abundant harvest of the simple peasant who "tastes" of the "blessed fruit of his labors" (189) and the "barren thickets" of the cultured individual whose harvest "edibles" all have "one taste." This basic opposition, assuming a variety of forms, was to become a traditional theme in nineteenth-century Russian literature.

In "Autumn" neither contradiction is unraveled. The poet's life, unlike the peasant's, is not to be crowned with satisfaction and well-being. Instead, he remains in his grave of solitude, trapped between the two outlets he has devised for himself. Setting forth each of these, he declines to choose. The pained flow of ideas is unexpectedly cut short, and the poem ends in a portrayal of inertia and stagnation.

Winter has arrived and the earth is transformed into "wide bald spots of impotence," including the fields which shone so gladly with their golden harvest. This picture bears a close affinity to the senile "winter" of the world in "The Last Poet," whereas the immobility—consequence of frenzied thought processes—brings to mind the conclusion of "The Last Death." Everything of the past year and indeed, of past life, is hidden under the snow of advancing winter and old age that covers the earth with an empty, deadening whiteness. The poet has no harvest to sustain himself, nor does he have hope of a "future harvest," a circumstance underscored by the last resounding "no!"

Assuming the status of a kind of spiritual biography, "Autumn," as "The Stillborn," is central to Baratynsky's poetry. As most of his major works, it posits uncompromising opposites that do not achieve resolution. Reminiscent especially of "The Last Death" and "The Last Poet" in its outcome and overtones of death and destruction, it is at once more intimate and introspective than these, and the scope of mental activity it encompasses is much broader. Built on the logical progression of thought like the two earlier poems, its perspective is more hopeless than either of these in that it portrays the poet himself, rather than beings exterior to him, slowly perishing as a result of inability either to escape from this endless progression or to fashion for himself a workable settlement.

As is characteristic of many of Baratynsky's most typical poems, it represents a continuation of the rationalistic technique of reflection, while at the same time revealing a deep desire to abandon it. In the last stanza the poet merges with the earth, symbol of his inner dissension here and in earlier lyrics. The image of the earth's "bald spots of impotence" is no less daring than the impotence symbolized by the aborted baby in "The Still-born." Therefore, he, too, will be stricken by the bleak shroud of snow, in the same way as his mind was paralyzed by nature's "sepulchral countenance" in "Where is the sweet whisper..." He faces this prospect, frightening in its inevitability, in dismal solitude.

The persistent course of thought is renewed in "Blessed is he who proclaimed a sacred essence!..." (Blagosloven svyatoe voz-vestivshiy!...), 1839. This short poem is sometimes interpreted as an endorsement of the Realistic method in literature and is suggestive of the ideas expressed in the preface to "The Gypsy Girl" and "Anticriticism" (Antikritika).[11] These ideas are verbalized here in archaic vocabulary and intricate syntax, the key to which lies in two past active participles (vozvestvshiy and obnazhivshiy) used as substantives.

The "evil inclination of human hearts" can be as instructive as "sacred" impulses. "Darkness" must be explored as well as "light," depravity, as well as goodness. This aspiration to penetrate to the extremes of personality and motivation recalls, in particular, the juxtaposition of the "revelations of Hades" and "celestial dreams" in "The Goblet." In a formal sense the alternation of light and dark is similar to the compositional technique of "Of what use are you, days!.." and "Disquieting day is pleasant to the crowd,..."

The last poem in Twilight, "Rhyme" (Rifma), 1840, echoes "The Last Poet" in theme and setting. The first part is imbued with a rhetorical intonation which harmonizes with the depiction of the Greek poet as an orator who lived one life with the people. The use of the image of harvest suggests the fullness of poetry and life: the poet, whose harmony flows forth as fields of full-ripe grain roll in the wind, is put in the same perspective as the "waves" of his fascinated listeners. They move together in one consonant motion, each evokes a response in the other. Syntactical parallelism, alliterative lines, lexical repetition, and varying lines of four and six-foot iambs affirm the expanse and richness of his "ample meter."

Conversely, these devices assist in confirming the fallen status of the modern poet. The change in emphasis, signified by the conjunction "but," is accompanied by the termination of the lilt and sweep of the six-foot lines and the introduction of a more matter-of-fact tonality and terminology. The modern poet is both the "judge" and the "accused" and is at a loss to decide whether his passion is a "ludicrous ailment" or a "higher gift." In a world which is almost a duplicate of that in "The Last Poet," poetry is the one consolation. As "sounds responding to sounds" elated the youth in "When I was young, with ringing call...," so it is rhyme · here which gives delight and a sign of life in a world filled with a "gravelike" chill.

Unlike the earlier poem, which had shown the poet on the verge of renouncing poetry altogether, "Rhyme" depicts poetry as providing the only solace in an age of declining poetic interests and values. It alone brings a "living twig" to the poet from his "native shore"; in his "ark" of isolation it alone soothes with the "divine impulse" of its response.

The opposition of the poet to society in "Rhyme" is a constantly recurring motif in *Twilight*. Closely intertwined with it is that inner struggle between contradictions that had always been present in Baratynsky's work and that was in large part responsible for the form in which this opposition is expressed. In endeavoring to resolve this inner struggle, he had found a fleeting and inconstant harmony in an exalted poetic world of earlier poems. In *Twilight* that endeavor is seldom made.

His conflicts are now seen as irresolvable and even identified with the special role of the poet. Poetry is no longer a higher place which triumphs over the base world of dissonant reality; rather it is a reality of rationalism, reflected in its partiality for utility, that overcomes poetry. This the poet cannot accept. Reason, frequently praised during the early years of his creativity, has become his implacable enemy. Accordingly, he retreats into a hopeless, dissension-ridden solitude, from which he is inclined to contemplate a world which he sees as swallowing up poetry. This solitude receives its highest expression in "The Last Poet," "The Stillborn," and "Autumn."

The title *Twilight*, as well as "Autumn," symbolizes this pervasive atmosphere of futility and disconsolation. Suggested in these concepts are the "twilight" and "autumn" of existence itself, an intervening time between day and night, summer and winter, a suspension between life and death. They also carry a recognition that life is passing without bringing the desired fulfillment and happiness. Intimately linked with this decline is that of the appreciation of poetry and art in an increasingly materialistic world. It is therefore a twilight of extraordinary weariness and despondency, the "swan song of Pushkin's generation, sung alone by Baratynsky, without the support of friends."[12]

As in the case of his two other collections, Baratynsky revised many of his poems in connection with their appearance in *Twilight*, but the revisions were much less extensive than before and consisted, for the most part, of isolated stylistic changes. Unlike these other editions, he achieved internal unity in *Twilight* to the extent that it represents an exceptional phenomenon in Russian literary practices of the time. Its structure, as well as its thematic title, was possibly modeled on French collections of the 1820's and 1830's. The title, in particular, recalls Victor Hugo's *Les chants du crépuscule* of 1835.[13]

Baratynsky's contemporaries, however, found nothing striking in the little collection. Belinsky, in his long, mostly negative article, which did much to influence the indifferent attitude of successive generations toward Baratynsky, did assign him "first place" of "all the poets, appearing together with Pushkin."[14]

Of the few other articles which were written, perhaps Shevyryov's note in the *Muscovite* is among the most interesting:

One is struck most of all in Ba—sky's *Twilight* by the spectacular change which has taken place in him: profound, concentrated melancholy—the fruit of life experience—has swept away all previous, buoyant, bright thoughts and feelings, has covered with the blackest shadow the lively image of his mature Muse, and alone, without any companions, without any other surroundings, has settled upon him. Such a metamorphosis in one of Pushkin's age is indeed a remarkable development and worthy of study.[15]

II *The Last Poems*

Toward the beginning of the 1840's when the former editors of the *Moscow Observer*, including Kireevsky and Shevyryov, began to organize the Slavophil periodical, the *Muscovite*, Baratynsky did not collaborate with them. Subsequently, in the polemics between this group and Belinsky, he suspected his former friends of intrigue against him, as well as against their adversaries.

The first poem to carry allusions to this intrigue was the epigram "To the Coterie" (*Kotterie*), 1842, which was deleted from *Twilight* by the censorship. It is apparently addressed to the *Muscovite* editors,[16] and its vehemence, indicative of the author's indignation, is climaxed in the last two lines by an ironic twisting of Christ's words to the apostles. Pushkin, working on his projected article on Baratynsky in 1830, had already noted his ability and artistry as a writer of epigrams.[17] The peculiarity of Baratynsky's late epigrams is that they transcend the biographical undercurrent which serves as a point of departure, to become expanded and generalized delineations, sharp and concentrated in their drawing of satirical character.

"Thank you, troublesome malice,..." (*Spasibo zlobe khlopotlivoy,...*), 1842, echoes the above epigram in both content and tangled syntactical structure, and gives a hint of Baratynsky's lack of participation in Moscow literary life. Like "To the Coterie" it incorporates a Biblical incident and recasts it to fit another context, in which animosity and irony are accentuated by repetition of "thank you." These epigrams have fundamental links with *Twilight*. The earlier opposition between the poet and the crowd has been narrowed to one between him and certain elements of the press. The same sense of enforced isolation and the concomitant embitterment have been retained, but the reaction is more incisive and biting.

These basic distinctions are reflected in "When your voice, O poet,..." (*Kogda, tvoy golos, O poet,...*), 1843, in which the first three stanzas constitute a series of rhetorical questions, succeeded by a negative rejoinder in the fourth. The Classically elevated depiction of the poet, similar to that of Goethe ("On the Death of Goethe") in its tones of ennoblement, gives way to the coarse and sinister image of the uncomprehending critic, who pronounces the requiem over the corpse "in order to touch the living" with his offensive censer. Whether the poet referred to is actually Lermontov or Pushkin, and the critic is Belinsky, loses significance in that the event is generalized to the point of universality.

Like features are perceptible in "On the Planting of a Wood" (*Na posev lesa*), 1843, which, however, transcends the style and scope of the epigrams, and has broader ties with *Twilight*. In this poem winter has passed, and with the coming of spring the fields are alive with activity as the peasants begin to plow with "submission and hope," just as the peasant in "Autumn" had "sown with hope" and dreamed of harvest time.

Unrewarded by a harvest himself, the poet has yet survived

his bleak winter, but it has been a survival without meaning and he is suspended in utter emptiness. As his body had gazed at the needless and endless succession of day and night in "Of what use are you, days!...," here it watches the vacant recurrence of the seasons. And, as in "Autumn," he draws a negative comparison between a peasant and himself, again shifting from a physical to a mental frame of reference and once more employing archaic vocabulary and rhythmic-syntactical parallelisms:

> But now there is no spring within my soul,
> But now within my soul there is no hope,
> The earthly world now passes from my sight,
> I lower my eyes before eternal day. (198)

Unlike "Autumn," where the concrete details of the woods and fields are transferred to an abstract plane, earthly landscape recedes from sight. The poet closes his eyes before "eternal day" and loses himself in a remote, ethereal place far from the transience and despondency of temporal reality in the same way that he had earlier envisioned an "unsetting day" and a "timeless spring."

The third stanza marks a return to the perspectives and movement of everyday actualities, and in contrast to the immobile winter described in the concluding stanza of "Autumn," where he could see no further than himself, he acknowledges that the winter which silvers his hair also holds within itself the seed of future generations. Moreover, he also realizes that he himself has not yet stepped over the "threshold of the earth," and he appeals to those from whom he so consistently isolated himself in *Twilight*.

The following stanzas are directly related to Baratynsky's epigrams of the time, but to just whom the "feasts of malevolence" and the digger of the "hidden pit" refer, remains unclear.[18] It would appear likely that Baratynsky was thinking of Belinsky, in the light of his preoccupation with the younger generation, for it is the latter who rewards the expression of his good wishes with silence, and he is bitter and angry at this lack of recognition. His frustration is reflected in the decision to renounce poetry and set out seeds of "fir trees, oaks, and pines."

More than twenty years earlier the poet had nurtured plans of planting a wood in "Home," and just as Pushkin was to do some time later in the poem beginning "Again I visited that little corner of the earth..." (*Vnov ya posetil tot ugolok zemli...*),

1835, he had looked forward with anticipation to the emergence of a new generation. He now plants his trees, but there is no trace of the enthusiasm and acceptance of change with which he had surrounded the project in his imagination. Rather, it is a defensive measure taken to assure himself of a return: denied a harvest in his "sowing" of poetic thoughts in "Autumn," he, emulating the peasant, turns to the soil and nature.

In the last stanza there is a mystical, Schelling-like connection made between nature and poetry, and the two members of the parallel he sets up, hopelessly disjointed in "Autumn," are synthesized at last. In abandoning the lyre, he transfers its secret powers to nature and thus ascertains that his poetry will live in majestic eternity. Filled with pessimism in regard to the rejection of his work by his contemporaries, he places his confidence in a faraway tomorrow, when his "mighty and gloomy children" (199) will attain to their full glory. The young Alcibiades and the old, repudiated poet ("What kind of rhymes?...") had also awaited a future immortality. In these poems the poet, unable to come to terms with his own time, opposes to it a more agreeable future, as he opposed a gratifying past to the disgrace of the present in "Rhyme."

"I love you, goddesses of poetry,..." (*Lyublyu ya vas, bogini penia,...*), 1844, carries a suggestion of the first of these nebulous consolations. Imbued with a personal tonality in the first stanza, the theme of incompatibility between inspiration and the hostile reception it occasions is subsequently generalized. Accompanying this expansion is an accumulation of archaic phraseology, which instills substance and gravity in the contradictory alliance between the "love of the muses" and the "animosity of Fortune." Enjambment and exclamation stress the resolve to relinquish the lyre.

He prefers to fall silent rather than awaken the gods of thunder and lightning, within whom his destiny sleeps. Torn between the caress of the muse and the desire to avoid the violence which ensues, he postpones the rendezvous until another day. And in mute and tormented seclusion he bides his time, contemplating the dubious possibility of a more favorable atmosphere for the acceptance of his poetry.

The poet turns to the eternal future in "The Prayer" (*Molitva*), 1842 or 1843. In this, Baratynsky's only poem in anapests, religious preoccupations are resumed. Life, noted as "ill" in the epistle

"To Delvig," has never really altered its status; the one who longed for "oblivion" in "Thought, thought alone!..." now prays for it. As before, he is entangled in the "delusions of earth," and he begs for the strength that will enable him to achieve a higher peace. Heaven is still an escape from the earth, but its lofty array of harps ("Autumn") is nonexistent in the sternness which it embodies in this short lyric of six lines. On the contrary, it is viewed as something approaching a last resort, and in crying for strength for the "heart," the prayer paradoxically recalls the first attempts to find peace in the "stern" lessons of reason.

The "flowering shore" hidden from the earth by a "black mist" remained an illusion, and "The Prayer" concludes Baratynsky's religous verse. More characteristic for him is the "doubt" voiced in "When, a child of passion and of doubt,..." (*Kogda, ditya i strasti i somnenia,...*), 1844. Written during the winter spent in Paris and addressed to his wife, this lyrical poem represents the final development of the motif of a "tender friend," which unfolds in a series of previous works. Further, "agitation" is again linked to the process of poetic creation and the allusion to the poetic "sacrament of sorrow" adds a last note to those poems in which that process acquires an aura of mystery and elevation. The unfailing tendency to posit unresolved opposites is pinpointed in the pairing of the vivid and chaotic "savage hell" and the vision of "paradise."

During the spring of 1844, while en route by ship from Marseilles to Naples, Baratynsky composed "The Steamer" (*Piroskaf*). Its descriptions of the sea and Italy bring to mind his youthful desire to join the navy and his lifelong fascination with the Classical world of ancient Italy. Comprised of six stanzas "The Steamer" is written in dactylic, with five instances of internal catalexis, all of which occur at the caesura (/--/- /--/).

The first three stanzas enthusiastically detail the beginning of the journey; the fourth is a subjective meditation, which contains an outburst of optimism having no precedents in Baratynsky's verse. Whether he had really settled the "rebellious questions" given expression in his poetry since its beginnings is doubtful, but it seemed so to him in his access of joy at being at sea and the immediate prospects of seeing Italy. The "hope" symbolized by the anchor infuses the remainder of the poem.

The buoyancy of "The Steamer" is not sustained in "To the Italian-Tutor" (*Dyadke-Italyantsu*), 1844, a long epistle dedicated

to Borghese, his tutor. Extended use of grammatical subordination
and inversion results in lengthy, difficult sentences very much like
those of "Autumn." Unified by the figure of Borghese the epistle
is concerned with the poet's earliest recollections as a child and
the visit to Naples. Included in the account of boyhood impressions
are the death of his father, Abram Andreevich, in Moscow and the
return to Mara, as well as a portrayal of Borghese, his devotion to
the family, and his predilection for recounting endless tales of Rome
and Naples, Suvorov and Napoleon. The sketch of Suvorov's death
in the Alps merges into that of the tutor's own and its effect on his
young charges, already "witnesses of the inconstancies of the earth."

At this point the stream of memories is replaced by the actuality
of Naples, perceived as a place of oblivion by one "alien to
oblivion." Suffused with the glory of its sunlight and suspended in purple mists and unfading greenery, it drowses in the
heat, lost in a dream of its past. The poetic desire to mingle the
"dream of delightful bliss" and the "last, eternal sleep" into a
"golden torpor" links the languor of the city with death and
makes of it a paradise of self-forgetfulness. Its immobility is caught
in the image of vines, "Whose nameless leaf has drooped so
faithfully its face,/Degraded long ago from its divinity,/And now
hangs half-asleep suspended from its brow" (204).

Byron is then pictured dragging "the poisons of his breast along
the burning shores" (204) of Italy in search of distraction from
"fatal thought." He, like the suffering Tantalus, fails in his
quest for oblivion. Borghese found oblivion in death, not in Italy,
but in distant, "icy" Russia, a land covered with the frosts and
snows of winter, as contrasted to Italy, which is filled with flowers
and fruits, and steeped in sunshine. The "storm-breathing" north
wind of the one, however, in the end blows with the same peace
as the "southern sighs" of the other's west wind.

"To the Italian-Tutor" was Baratynsky's last poem. It may be
noted once again that, in general, his post-*Twilight* verse reveals
organic ties with *Twilight* and with his poetry as a whole. The
device of opposing the poet to his surroundings, immediately connected with *Twilight*, has its ultimate sources in such early elegies
as "Finland" and "Dejection," as well as in later lyrics, including
"To Imitators" and "To Yazykov."

Unlike *Twilight*, Baratynsky's last poems contain scattered suggestions of reconciliation in regard to the conflicts that penetrated his work. In "On the Planting of a Wood," he, at least,

acknowledges directly the rise of a new generation, the disjunction
between himself and that generation notwithstanding. Moreover,
the deep rift in "Autumn" that separated the poet from his antithesis, the peasant, is healed in the identification of poetry and
the grove of trees. "The Steamer" is the single most affirmative
poem in all of his mature verse; but the absence of this note in the
epistle to Borghese, which resurrects the search for oblivion, indicates that perhaps it was but the product of a temporary and isolated
circumstance.

Conclusion

O pposite means of perception and thought found expression in Baratynsky's early poetry in the collision of "feeling" and "reason." This clash was not unusual in the decades of reaction which followed eighteenth-century rationalism. Rather, the atmosphere of actuality, testifying to a substantial and genuine inner division, penetrates many of his elegies and epistles, and thus sets them apart. Corresponding to the character of such a conflict is his rationalistic procedure of poetic reflection, manifested in the positing of thesis and antithesis.

In many of his best and most typical romantic elegies, the negative component, that is, the appeal to reason, is uppermost and inspires moods of resignation and weariness. The aura of detachment, developed in subtle psychological tonalities, received its ultimate extension in "Of what use are you, days!..." whereas the theme of love itself practically disappeared in his lyrics towards the middle of the 1820's.

In another group of elegies characterized by abstractness and elevated intonation, opposition is delineated in separate contexts. These range from "Finland," where the agitation of a remote past is contrasted to the silence of the present, to "The Skull," which is concerned with the discrepancy between life and death, and from the preferred inactivity of "Two Fates" to the chaotic thirst for action of "The Storm." In "To Delvig" inner dissension embraces the incompatibility of heaven and earth. All of these are interrelated and may be seen as expansions of the basic collision between emotion and rationality.

Baratynsky's tendency to reflect and analyze gives his verse a dry, abstract quality. His inclination to carry logic to its extreme is perhaps best exemplified by "The Last Death." During the latter half of the 1820's his poetry began to evince signs of a deep desire to escape the lack of accord engendered by endless dialectics. It was also during these years that he came under the lasting influence of the Russian partisans of Schelling, who promoted esthetics at the expense of logic and rationalism. Thus, in time, poetry came to embody for Baratynsky a remote place of harmony and beauty, a retreat from inner controversy.

This theme had been foreshadowed in the art-for-art motifs of earlier poems, but it now attained a higher and fuller expression in a series of lyrics devoted to art as salvation. The device of opposition received a new development and dimension in the juxtaposition of the exalted world of poetry with unpleasant, confused reality. Neither the "wondrous city" of art nor the possibility of a religious outlet, however, proved to more than temporary consolation, and Baratynsky failed to project a consistently positive outlook. Documenting the failure were intensified preoccupations with death, as well as accelerated moods of melancholy, determinism, and the continuing subjugation to the rationalistic process of thought.

The constant decline of his popularity toward the beginning of the 1830's was augmented by the appearance of "Eda," "The Ball," and "The Gypsy Girl." In each of these he was unsuccessful in imposing balance and harmony on the opposing tendencies of his compositional method. Too, all three bore the strong, unassimilated influence of Pushkin. In the final analysis the genre of the long poem as a whole remained beyond his grasp: the merits of their separate technical aspects notwithstanding, they are, in large part, unoriginal and less interesting than his lyric verse.

The poems of *Twilight* represent a reflection of Baratynsky's mature disillusionment, consequence of the inability to harmonize contradictory principles. Here the opposition of the poet to society, prefigured in other works, is expanded to that between spiritual culture and commercialism. Such is the leitmotif of *Twilight*.

Within *Twilight* "The Stillborn" extends inner lack of accord to a universal scale encompassing eternity in its all-inclusiveness. Another of Baratynsky's greatest poems is "Autumn," which, as "The Stillborn," is connected with the main body of his poetic achievement. Both of these pinpoint and symbolize an intervening position between absolutes, and ultimately, a sense of belonging nowhere. As the "stillborn" is suspended between life and death, heaven and earth, the poet himself is transfixed between summer and winter in "Autumn," between day and night in *Twilight*.

And in this grey half-world of decline and impending darkness, he continues to grapple with opposing outlooks as before. The distinction is that he creates an atmosphere symbolizing both a midway attitude, an indefinite point somewhere between extremes, and a recognition of failure and frustration, a "twilight" of pessimism and misery.

The pinnacle of Baratynsky's originality in this regard is the personal symbol of the "stillborn." In the ambiguous status of the aborted child he concentrates and visualizes all of the ambiguity and uncertainty of his thought, and his consequent feelings of insignificance and powerlessness. Essentially modernist in conception and execution, the half-soul of the "still-born," held in abeyance between paradise and earthly reality, capsules and eternizes the basis of a mentality beset by conflict and doubt. A contradiction in itself, it becomes a symbol of perpetual inner contradiction.

Baratynsky's narrowing creative perspectives, which had shown a gradual compression since the early 1830's, are especially apparent in the post-*Twilight* poems. This petrifaction, as it were, which Pushkin escaped completely, tended to be typical of those Russian poets who were still alive in the late thirties and forties of the last century. Yazykov's verse, for instance, lost its early enthusiasm and gravitated toward empty praises of a Slavophile brand of nationalism. Such a trend was characteristic of Vyazemsky, above all, whose isolation and resentment were prolonged by his long life (1792-1878). The bright prospects of the 1820's were by now irretrievably lost to these, and in an artistic milieu which had little use for them or their verse culture, they became increasingly stationary and shut off from current directions in literature.

Broader in scope in its initial years, Baratynsky's poetry, in general, does not lack positive moods. These are implicit in his conventional epicurean motifs, certain of his romantic elegies, the images of a "tender friend," and traditional praises of a quiet happiness. Beyond these he turned to art—which he often sought to identify with nature—for harmony.

In the long run, however, irresolution and unresolved contrasts are far more characteristic of him than volition and synthesis. Forever immersed in oppositions with diverse connotations, he projects his duality into all of life and even the afterlife. At the basis of this duality lay the conflict between inherent individual sensitiveness and impressibility and the reasoning proclivities imposed by a rationalistic education.

Reason was always a limiting factor for him, an entity which constrained and impeded the spontaneous motion of passion and imagination. In his early poems the earth came to symbolize the confinement of reason, whereas in his later work, the earth is a symbol of the inner struggle between reason and feeling. In a similar way his images of paradise evolved from a home of fantasy and romance to a place where opposing principles were balanced and synthesized.

In *Twilight* discord is complete, and it is here that Baratynsky's duality receives its most pointed clarity and its most indelible expression. Being in substance far more profound than the internal division and contradictory impulses of many of Lermontov's lyrical personae, for example, as well as of Pechorin, the poetic reflection of this remarkably inconsistent frame of mind, with its concern for precision in phraseology, is extraordinary in the history of Russian poetry. Unlike the poetry of Pushkin, Lermontov, and Tyutchev, Baratynsky's work, with a few minor exceptions,[1] contains no stirring pieces on politics or the motherland.

Despite the Romanticism of his various themes, he remained strongly tied to eighteenth-century Classicism in form, which imposed order and restraint, and effected a logical treatment of lyrical subject matter. Apart from form, much of Baratynsky's early poetry bears the influence of the French rationalism in which he was educated. Even after he abandoned the appeals to reason, his poetic thought clung to both the method and style inherent to rationalist poetry. Thus, the content of his later work, while intellectual in atmosphere and technique, lacks the thematic rationality of much of the work that preceded it.

Intellectualism, typical of his verse and thought, distinguishes Baratynsky from the other Petersburg poets, including those, who, as Pushkin and Delvig, were essentially Classicists in attitude and form. Having its roots in French abstract poetry, Baratynsky's intellectualism retained its individuality throughout the twenty-five years of his poetic activity and was largely responsible for the designation of "the poet of thought," assigned him by many Russian critics and literary historians.

His intellectualism is permeated by the ever-present duality, apparent in the dialectical juxtaposition of opposites and in the contradictory features of an unending pattern of analytical meditation: the intense activity of its method and the inertia of its unrelenting persistence. Intellectualism accounts for the double significance of many of his images, which tend to point to a process of thought behind the visual picture. Moreover, it determines the peculiarly static traits not only of the images, but of the delicate tracing of the most refined nuances of emotion.

Finally, intellectualism contributes to the philosophical qualities, embodied in breadth of generalization and rhetorical intonation, which accrue to his mature work and, in particular, to *Twilight*. These qualities in no way indicate the existence of a consistent philosophical system. The conflicts with which his poetry is preoccupied spring from an individual rather than a philosophical context. Not enthusiastic about Kireevsky's interpretation of Schelling's idealism *per se*, Baratynsky retained an enduring fascination with certain of its motifs. In this sense there was neither strategy nor design in his lyrics, as was the case, for instance, in the poems of Venevitinov, one of Schelling's ardent Russian partisans.

A factor lending both intellectual and philosophical properties to Baratynsky's later verse, especially, is his syntactical complexity. Corresponding in many cases to a parallel complexity in the flow of poetic thought, this syntax adds sharp precision and compressed intensity to that flow. It mirrors the basically analytical mentality of which it is an expression. The product of a mind trained in reason, it is inclined at times to carry grammatical logic of subordination and agreement to logical extremes, even as thought itself is frequently developed to its ultimate and logical maximum. This tendency is best illustrated in *Twilight*, but complicated phrases make their way into his work as early as the second half of the 1820's. It distinguished his poetry from that of the other poets of the time, to whom the practice was alien, and it continues to be an exceptional phenomenon in the whole of Russian poetry.

Connected with intricate expression and investing it with solemnity is the use of Church Slavonic terminology. This habit was modified from the simple inclusion of conventional archaisms and turns of speech in his early verse to the usage, in the 1830's and thereafter, of words which had long since ceased to appear in poetry. The appearance of antiquated vocabulary in the poem "Death" was only one of the earliest and most conspicuous examples of a trend which found its most concentrated application in "Autumn."

As the complex syntax which it complements, this turn to archaic language in the 1830's was unprecedented. It can be seen as a kind of psychological defense, and linked with his solitude and isolation, with the attempt to elevate the role of poet as opposed to the apparent coarseness of the public. In the light of his disjunction with the times, it can further be perceived as a need to identify with the past and, notably, with the Classicism of the preceding century, when such language was characteristic of poetry and when poetry constituted the major literary expression of an entire age.

Typical of Baratynsky, however, is the fact that alongside this lofty terminology appeared prosaic and commonplace words, many of which were taken from the journalese of the period. These contrasts in linguistic levels often reinforce the discrepancies between planes of thought or function to point up the gravity or irony of the ideas they voice. Related to this tendency is Baratynsky's partiality for neologisms and compound word formations, many formed from archaic elements of speech. Further, these are often prefixed by negatives, which accentuate a positive concept.

Also adding color and freshness to his poetic language is an extensive accumulation of unusual adjectives. Vivid epithets were common to many of Baratynsky's contemporaries, as well as to Derzhavin; but in a succession of poems containing attributives rare for poetry, which range from "Dissuasion" through "The Last Death" to "On the Planting of a Wood," Baratynsky instilled into his verse a singularity unmistakably his. Many of his rhymes are likewise imbued with crisp novelty, and with few exceptions, all of them adhere to a high standard of exactness.

Metrically, Baratynsky was a skilled and consummate practitioner of the iambic tetrameter, a meter for which he nourished a special preference. Of his 230 lyric poems, 202 are in iambic, and of this number, 105 are in iambic tetrameter—as well as six of the long poems. His propensity to leave the first foot unstressed set him apart even in a time when this practice was popular in the iambic tetrameter, for he carried it to a greater extent than any other poet: fully 9.4% of his first-foot stresses are omitted, and only Karolina Pavlova approaches a comparable percentage (8.1%). Corresponding to the high number of pyrrhics in the first foot is the low number of second-foot pyrrhics (1.7%), the lowest of the poets of Pushkin's time.[2]

Overshadowed by Pushkin, Baratynsky remains significantly original and a master in his own right. Pushkin himself was sensitively aware of the individual features of Baratynsky's poetry as early as 1830, and he wrote in a projected article:

Baratynsky belongs to the number of our excellent poets. With us he is original, for he thinks. He would be original everywhere, for he thinks in his own way, truly and independently, while he feels intensely and deeply. The harmony of his verse, the freshness of his style, the verve and precision of expression must impress everyone, even someone poorly endowed with taste and feeling.[3]

Discarded and largely ignored, however, by the great majority of the critics and the public long before his death, Baratynsky's work lay half-forgotten and unread, for the most part, for over fifty years. Only toward the end of the century when Russian poetry was experiencing a new era of competence and brilliance was it rediscovered and reevaluated by the Russian Symbolists, especially Bryusov. Apart from Bryusov's articles and those of other writers, editions of Baratynsky's poetry appeared again and again, culminating with the publication in 1914-1915 of the two-volume *Complete Works* by the Imperial Academy of Sciences.

And Baratynsky continues to be appreciated more in the twentieth than in the preceding century, both in the Soviet Union and in the West. Unlike Pushkin, who is valued for his poetry, as well as his drama, prose, and literary criticism, Baratynsky's worth is measured today by his relatively small volume of poetry alone, and of this, by his lyric verse, above all. Thus it is perhaps ironic that more direct reflections of his poetry than of Pushkin's were to appear in the development of subsequent Russian verse, and they can be traced from Tyutchev through Sluchevsky, Annensky, and Blok to Pasternak, among others.

Baratynsky's persistent dualism, his adeptness in psychological depiction, his profound disillusionment, his symbolism, together with the intellectual, immobile character of his verse and its syntactic complexity—all these distinctive qualities reserve for him a unique and special place, not only in the history of Russian poetry, but in that of European poetry in its entirety.

Notes And References

CHAPTER ONE

1. N. V. Gogol', *Vybrannye mesta iz perepiski s druz'iami*, in *Polnoe sobranie sochinenii*, VII (1952), 385-86.

2. E. A. Boratynskii. *Materialy k ego biografii*. With introduction and notes of Iurii Verkhovskii (Petrograd, 1916), p. 26.

3. *Ibid.*, p. 26.

4. *Ibid.*, pp. 27-28.

5. "Pis'ma E. A. Baratynskogo k N. V. Putiate," *Russkii arkhiv*, V, No. 2 (1867), 264.

6. E. A. Boratynskii, *Stikhotvoreniia, poemy, proza, pis'ma* (Moscow, 1951), pp. 483-84.

7. In A. S. Pushkin, *Polnoe sobranie sochinenii* (1937), XIII, 276.

8. *Sochineniia Evgeniia Abramovicha Baratynskogo* (Moscow, 1869), p. 439.

9. *Stikhotvoreniia*, 1951, p. 500.

10. A. S. Pushkin, *Polnoe sobranie sochinenii v desiati tomakh*, 3rd ed. (Moscow, 1962-1966), X, 334.

11. *Stikhotvoreniia*, 1951, p. 516.

12. *Ibid.*, p. 520.

13. *Ibid.*, p. 521.

14. *Ibid.*, p. 528.

15. M. Longinov, "Baratynskii i ego sochineniia," *Russkii arkhiv*, No. 2 (1867), 262.

CHAPTER TWO

1. Yurii Tynianov, "Arkhaisty i Pushkin," *Arkhaisty i novatory* (Leningrad, 1929), p. 138.

2. M. Gofman, *Poeziia Boratynskogo; istoriko-literaturnyi etiud* (Petrograd, 1915), pp. 7-8.

3. K. N. Batiushkov, *Polnoe sobranie stikhotvorenii,* 2nd ed. (Moscow-Leningrad, 1964), p. 222.

4. I. L. Al'mi, "Elegii E. A. Baratynskogo 1819-1824 godov," *Voprosy istorii literatury.* Gertsen State Pedagogical Institute of Leningrad, 219 (1961), 37.

5. Pointed out by L. Ginsburg, "Lirika Baratynskogo," *Russkaia literatura,* II (1964), 30.

6. E. N. Kupreianova, "E. A. Baratynskii," in E. A. Baratynskii, *Polnoe sobranie stikhotvorenii,* 2nd ed. (Leningrad, 1957), p. 18.

7. Al'mi, 41, and Ginsburg, 30.

8. I. Medvedeva, "Sbornik stikhotvorenii 1827 g.," in E. A. Baratynskii, *Polnoe sobranie stikhotvorenii* (Moscow-Leningrad, 1936), I, 342-43.

9. Kupreianova, "E. A. Baratynskii," *Polnoe,* 1957, p. 17.

10. See N. R. Mazepa, *E. A. Baratynskii. Esteticheskie i literaturno-kriticheskie vzgliady* (Kiev, 1960), p. 73.

11. Pushkin, 3rd ed., III, 30.

12. In a speech of June 13, 1821, given at a meeting of the Society of the Lovers of Russian Literature. See Kupreianova, "Primechaniia," *Polnoe,* 1957, p. 344.

13. In *Mnemozina,* Part II (1824), 42.

14. E. Malkina in "Finliandskaia povest' Baratynskogo," *Literaturnaia ucheba,* No. 2 (1939), 47-72, discusses in detail the relationships between Baratynskii's epistle and Kiukhel'beker's article and connects the latter with "Eda."

15. In Pushkin, *Polnoe* (1937), XIII, 108.

16. Gofman, *Poeziia Boratynskogo,* pp. 26-27.

17. For distinctions between Baratynskii's and Pushkin's poetic images of Zakrevskaia, see Iu. Ivask, "Boratynskii," *Novyi zhurnal,* L (1957), 143.

18. B. V. Tomashevskii, "Tropy," *Stilistika i stikhoslozhenie* (Leningrad, 1959), pp. 226-27.

19. Medvedeva, "Sbornik stikhotvorenii 1827 g.," 347-48.

20. In *Polnoe sobranie sochinenii* (St. Petersburg, 1914-1915), II, 212.

21. *Stikhotvoreniia,* 1951, p. 491.

22. For a more complete discussion of Baratynskii's revisions, see Gofman, "Rabota Boratynskogo nad ego stikhotvoreniiami," *Polnoe* (1914-1915), II, 279-95.

CHAPTER THREE

1. *Evgenii Onegin*, chapter three, stanza thirty, in Pushkin, 3rd ed., V, 68.

2. For a brief discussion of the coincidence of several features in "Piry" and Viazemskii's "Partizanu poetu" (1815), and of their subsequent expression in chapter four of *Evgenii Onegin*, see V. S. Nechaeva, "Iz arkhiva Boratynskogo," *Utrenniki* (Petrograd, 1922), 1, 69-71. For connections between "Piry" and Millevoye's "Le déjeuner," "Ruslan i Liudmila" and Pushkin, in general, see Gofman, "Poemy B—go," *Russkaia starina*, 161 (1915), 120-21.

3. For major differences between "Eda" and "Kavkazskii plennik," see Kupreianova, "E. Baratynskii," in E. A. Baratynskii, *Stikhotvoreniia*, 2nd ed. (Leningrad, 1948), pp. xxvii-xxix.

4. L. Andreevskaia, "Poemy Baratynskogo," *Russkaia poeziia XIX veka* (Leningrad, 1929), pp. 88-89.

5. Gofman, *Poeziia Boratynskogo*, p. 17.

6. V. G. Belinskii, "Literaturnye mechtaniia," *Polnoe sobranie sochinenii* (Moscow, 1953-1959), I, 74.

7. Pushkin, 3rd ed., X, 201-2.

8. *Ibid.*, VII, 83.

9. *Ibid.*, VII, 224.

10. "Iz bumag poeta I. I. Kozlova," *Russkii arkhiv*, XXIV (1886), 187.

11. In a letter to A. Iazykov, *Iazykovskii arkhiv*, II, No. I (1913), 243.

12. In Pushkin, *Polnoe* (1937), XIII, 149-50.

13. I. Medvedeva, "Rannii Baratynskii," *Polnoe* (1936), I, lxxi.

14. For other similarities (i.e., the rhyme of "Arsenii" with "Evgenii," recurrence of the name "Ol'ga" in Baratynskii's poem, etc.) see D. Mirsky, "Baratynskii," *Polnoe* (1936), I, xviii-xix.

15. Pushkin, 3rd ed., VII, 83.

16. I. V. Kireevskii, "Obozrenie russkoi slovesnosti za 1829 g.," *Polnoe sobranie sochinenii* (Moscow, 1911), II, 30.

17. *Stikhotvoreniia*, 1951, p. 493.

18. Kireevskii, "Obozrenie russkoi slovesnosti za 1831 g.," *Polnoe*, II, 47-54.

19. "Nalozhnitsa. Soch. E. Baratynskogo," *Literaturnaia gazeta*, No. 27 (May 11, 1831), 220-21.

20. Pushkin, 3rd ed., X, 332.

21. In "Pis'ma E. A. Boratynskogo k I. V. Kireevskomu (1829-

1833)," *Tatevskii sbornik S. A. Rachinskogo* (St. Petersburg, 1899), p. 28.

22. Belinskii, "Stikhotvoreniia E. Baratynskogo," *Polnoe*, VI, 485.

23. N. I. Nadezhdin, "'Nalozhnitsa,' sochinenie E. Baratynskogo," *Teleskop*, No. 10, Part III (1831), 228-39.

24. "Antikritika," in *Polnoe* (1914-1915), II, 213-23.

25. *Tatevskii sbornik*, p. 29.

26. *Stikhotvoreniia*, 1951, p. 495.

27. D. S. Mirsky, "Baratynsky," *A History of Russian Literature from its Beginnings to 1900*, ed. Francis J. Whitfield (New York, 1961), p. 104.

28. V. Zhirmunskii, "Pushkin i ego podrazhateli," *Bairon i Pushkin* (Leningrad, 1924), p. 239.

CHAPTER FOUR

1. *Stikhotvoreniia*, 1951, p. 484.

2. René Wellek, "The Early Romantics in Germany. Schelling," *A History of Modern Criticism: 1750-1950* (New Haven, 1955), II, 74.

3. *Ibid.*, 75.

4. *Ibid.*, 76.

5. *Stikhotvoreniia*, 1951, p. 486.

6. Tomashevskii, pp. 218-19.

7. Kireevskii, "Obozrenie russkoi slovesnosti za 1831 g.," *Polnoe*, II, 50.

8. Wellek, 76.

9. See, for example, "Materialy dlia biografii E. A. Baratynskogo," *Sochineniia*, 1869. p. 394.

10. Mirsky, "Baratynskii," *Polnoe* (1936), I, xxvii.

11. *Ibid.*, xxviii.

12. Gofman, "Primechaniia k stikhotvoreniiam," *Polnoe* (1914-1915), I, 288.

13. *Stikhotvoreniia*, 1951, p. 521.

CHAPTER FIVE

1. K. V. Pigarev, *Muranovo. Pamiatka ekskursanta* (Moscow, 1963), p. 28.

2. *Evropeets*, No. 1 (1832), 15.

3. Belinskii, "Stikhotvoreniia E. Baratynskogo," *Polnoe*, VI, 466-71.

4. *Istoriia russkoi literatury v trekh tomakh*, ed. D. D. Blagoi (Moscow-Leningrad, 1963), II, 472.

5. Ginsburg, 35.

6. Kupreianova, "Primechaniia," *Polnoe*, 1957, p. 370.

7. Ginsburg, 33.

8. Pointed out by Gleb Struve, "Evgeny Baratynsky," *The Slavonic and East European Review*, XXIII, No. 62 (January, 1945), 113.

9. *Ibid.*, 113.

10. *Istoriia russkoi literatury v trekh tomakh*, II, 300.

11. Pointed out by Mazepa, pp. 17, 19.

12. N. Kotliarevskii, "Zvezda rasroznennoi Pleiady" *Starinnye portrety* (St. Petersburg, 1907), p. 53.

13. Kupreianova, "Sumerki," *Polnoe* (1936), I, 356.

14. Belinskii, "Stikhotvoreniia E. Baratynskogo," *Polnoe*, VI, 479.

15. S. Shevyrev, "Kriticheskii perechen' proizvedenii Russkoi Slovesnosti za 1842 god," *Moskvitianin*, No. 1 (1843), 280.

16. Kupreianova, "Kommentarii k stikhotvoreniiam," *Polnoe* (1936), II, 279-80.

17. Pushkin, 3rd ed., VII, 223.

18. In a letter to Ia. K. Grot in 1846, Pletnev explained that the "hidden pit" was an allusion to the "dirty tricks" (*pakosti*) played on Baratynskii by the "young litterateurs," i.e., Belinskii and his Moscow colleagues, whereas "horns" (mentioned in the same stanza of Baratynskii's poem) signified a "fool." See *Perepiska Ia. K. Grota s P. A. Pletnevym* (St. Petersburg, 1896), II, 728-29. V. Briusov essentially agreed, but linked Baratynsky's mood specifically with his reaction to Belinskii's criticism of *Sumerki*; see "E. A. Baratynskii," *Novyi entsiklopedicheskii slovar'* (St. Petersburg), V, 178. On the other hand, the Soviet scholar Kupreianova believes that Baratynskii was referring to the *Moskvitianin* editors; see "Kommentarii," 375.

CONCLUSION

1. See, for instance, the epigram on Arakcheev ("Otchizny vrag, sluga tsaria, . . ."), *Polnoe*, 1957, p. 116.

2. All percentages are quoted from L. I. Timofeev, *Problemy stikhovedeniia. Materialy k sotsiologii stikha* (Moscow, 1931), pp. 213-14.

3. Pushkin, 3rd ed., VII, 221.

Selected Bibliography

PRIMARY SOURCES

Stikhotvoreniia (Poems). Moscow: Tipografiia Avgusta Semena, pri Imperatorskoi Mediko-Khirurgicheskoi Akademii, 1827.

Stikhotvoreniia (Poems). Moscow: Tipografiia Avgusta Semena, pri Imperatorskoi Mediko-Khirurgicheskoi Akademii, 1835.

Sumerki (Twilight). Moscow: Tipografiia Avgusta Semena, pri Imperatorskoi Mediko-Khirurgicheskoi Akademii, 1842.

Sochineniia (Works). Moscow, 1869.

Sochineniia (Works). 4th edition. Kazan': Univ. Tipografiia, 1884.

Polnoe sobranie sochinenii (Complete Works). Kiev: F. A. Ioganson, 1894.

Polnoe sobranie sochinenii (Complete Works). St. Petersburg: E. Pavlova, 1894.

Polnoe sobranie sochinenii (Complete Works), ed. I. N. Bozherianov. St. Petersburg: M. K. Remesova, 1894.

Polnoe sobranie sochinenii (Complete Works), edited and with notes by M. L. Gofman. Two volumes. St. Petersburg: Imperatorskaia Akademiia Nauk, 1914-1915.

Poety pushkinskoi pory (Poets of Pushkin's Time), edited and with introductory article by Iu. Verkhovskii. Moscow: M. i S. Sabashnikovy, 1919.

Izbrannye sochineniia (Selected Works), with introductory article and notes by M. L. Gofman. Berlin: Z. I. Grzhebin, 1922.

Polnoe sobranie stikhotvorenii (Complete poems), edited and with commentaries and biographical articles by E. Kupreianova and I. Medvedeva; introductory article by D. Mirsky. Two vols. Moscow-Leningrad: Sovetskii pisatel' (Biblioteka poeta, Bol'shaia seriia), 1936.

Stikhotvoreniia (Poems), edited and with introductory article and

notes by E. Kupreianova. Leningrad: Sovetskii pisatel' (Biblioteka poeta, Malaia seriia), 1937).

Stikhotvoreniia (Poems), edited and with introductory article
and notes by I. Medvedeva. Moscow: Goslitizdat, 1945.

Stikhotvoreniia (Poems), edited and with introductory article and
notes by E. Kupreianova. 2nd edition. Leningrad: Sovetskii
pisatel' (Biblioteka poeta, Malaia seriia), 1948).

*Stikhotvoreniia, poemy, proza, pis'ma (Poems, Long Poems, Prose,
Letters)*, preparation of text and notes by O. Muratova and K.
V. Pigarev; introductory article by K. V. Pigarev. Moscow:
Goslitizdat, 1951.

Polnoe sobranie stikhotvorenii (Complete Poems), introductory
article, preparation of text and notes by E.N. Kupreianova.
2nd edition. Leningrad: Sovetskii pisatel' (Biblioteka poeta,
Bol'shaia seriia), 1957.

Stikhotvoreniia i poemy (Poems and Long Poems), introductory
article, preparation of text and notes by L. A. Ozerov. 3rd edition. Leningrad: Sovetskii pisatel' (Biblioteka poeta, Malaia
seriia), 1958.

Lirika (Lyrics), compiled and with preface by K. Pigarev. Moscow:
Khudozhestvennaia literatura, 1964.

SECONDARY SOURCES

ADRIANOV, S. "Baratynskii," *Russkii biograficheskii slovar' (Russian Biographical Dictionary)*, ed. A. A. Polovtsov, Vol. II. St.
Petersburg: Imperatorskoe russkoe istoricheskoe obshchestvo,
1900. Contains a short biography and a simplified survey of
Baratynskii's major themes.

AIKHENVAL'D, IULII. "Baratynskii," *Siluety russkikh pisatelei (Sil-
houettes of Russian Writers)*, 4th edition, Vol. 1. Moscow: Mir,
1914. Short, but excellent discussion of Baratynskii's poetry.

AL'MI, I. L. "Elegii E. A. Baratynskogo 1819-1824 godov" ("Bara-
tynskii's Elegies from 1819-1824"), *Voprosy istorii literatury
(Problems of Literary History)*. A. I. Gertsen State Pedagogical
Institute of Leningrad, 219 (1961). Very interesting essay on
Baratynskii's early elegies against the literary background of the
Russian elegy, in general.

ANDREEVSKAIA, L. "Poemy Baratynskogo" ("Baratynskii's Long
Poems"), *Russkaia poeziia XIX veka (Russian Poetry of the
XIX Century)*. Leningrad: Academia, 1929. Devoted to a sur-

vey of Baratynskii's longer works, with emphasis on their psychological aspects.

ANDREEVSKII, S. A. "Poeziia Baratynskogo" ("Baratynskii's Poetry"), *Literaturnye ocherki (Literary Essays)*, 4th edition. St. Petersburg: Tipografiia A. S. Suvorina, 1913. One of the articles to reevaluate Baratynskii's work after decades of neglect on the part of Russian criticism.

BATIUSHKOV, F.D. "E.A. Baratynskii," *Istoriia russkoi literatury XIX veka (History of Russian Literature of the XIX Century)*, ed. D.N. Ovsianiko-Kulikovskii, Vol. II. Moscow: Mir, 1910. A brief discussion revealing nothing essentially interesting.

BEISOV, P. S. "Vospominaniia N. Konshina o Baratynskom" ("N. Konshin's Recollections of Baratynskii"), *Ruskaia literatura (Russian Literature)*, No. 3 (1959). Deals with the relationship between Baratynskii and the minor poet, Nikolai Konshin.

BELINSKII, V. G. "O stikhotvoreniiakh g. Baratynskogo" ("On the Poems of Mr. Baratynskii"), *Polnoe sobranie sochinenii (Complete Works)*, Vol. 1. Moscow: Akademiia nauk SSSR, 1953. A short, mostly negative article.

———. "Russkaia literatura v 1844 godu" ("Russian Literature in 1844"), *Polnoe sobranie sochinenii (Complete Works)*, Vol. VIII. Moscow: Akademiia nauk SSSR, 1955. Brief notes on Baratynskii's poetic thought.

———. "Stikhotvoreniia E. Baratynskogo" ("The Poems of E. Baratynskii"), *Polnoe sobranie sochinenii (Complete Works)*, Vol. VI. Moscow: Akademiia nauk SSSR, 1955. Lengthy, comprehensive, and largely negative in approach, this article was written in connection with the appearance of *Twilight* in 1842.

BELYI, ANDREI. "Opyt kharakteristiki russkogo chetyrekhstopnogo iamba ("An Attempt to Characterize Russian Iambic Tetrameter"), *Simvolizm (Symbolism)*. Moscow: Musaget, 1910. Contains interesting metrical material on many Russian poets, including Baratynskii.

———. "Pushkin, Tiutchev i Baratynskii v zritel'nom vospriiatii prirody" ("Pushkin, Tiutchev and Baratynskii and Visual Perception of Nature"), *Poeziia slova (Poetry of the Word)*. Petersburg: Epokha, 1922. The portion dealing with Baratynskii is fanciful and misleading.

BLAGOI, D. D. "Baratynskii," *Istoriia russkoi literatury v trekh tomakh (History of Russian Literature in Three Volumes)*,

Vol. II. Moscow: Akademiia nauk SSSR, 1963. Reliable survey of Baratynskii's work.

————. "Baratynskii," *Literaturnaia entsiklopediia (Literary Encyclopedia)*, ed. V. Friche, Vol. I. Moscow: Kommunisticheskaia akademiia, 1929. Reliable survey article.

BRIUSOV, VALERII IA. "Baratynskii," *Novyi entsiklopedicheskii slovar' (New Encyclopedic Dictionary)*, Vol. V. St. Petersburg: F. A. Brokgaus i P. A. Efron. Brief survey of life and works.

————. "Baratynskii i Sal'eri ("Baratynskii and Salieri"), *Russkii arkhiv (Russian Archives)*, No. 8 (1900). On the relationship between Baratynskii and Pushkin; refutes the idea that Pushkin's Salieri (in *Mozart and Salieri)* is a reflection of Baratynskii.

————. "K stoletiiu so dnia rozhdeniia E. A. Baratynskogo" ("Commemorating the 100th Anniversary of the Birth of E. A. Baratynskii"), *Russkii arkhiv (Russian Archives)*, No. 4 (1900). A general discussion including quotations from critical articles of the early 1830's on "The Gypsy Girl."

————. "Pushkin i Baratynskii" ("Pushkin and Baratynskii"), *Russkii arkhiv (Russian Archives)*, No. 1 (1901). On the personal relationship between the two poets.

————. "Staroe o G-ne Shcheglove" ("Something Old about Mr. Shcheglov"), *Russkii arkhiv (Russian Archives)*, No. 12 (1901). On the personal relationship between Baratynskii and Pushkin; also contains interesting remarks on the basic contradictions in Baratynskii's poetry.

BUNIN, IVAN. "E. A. Baratynskii," *Vestnik vospitaniia (Educational Bulletin)*, No. 6 (June, 1900). Rambling and unexciting.

E. A. Boratynskii. Materialy k ego biografii (E. A. Boratynskii. Materials for his Biography), with introduction and notes of Iu. Verkhovskii. Petrograd: Tipografiia Imperatorskoi Akademii Nauk, 1916. Biography; includes Baratynskii's early letters (in French) to his relatives.

FILIPPOVICH, P. P. *Zhizn' i tvorchestvo E. A. Baratynskogo (The Life and Works of E. A. Baratynskii)*. Kiev, 1917. A valuable and detailed reference work; has partial bibliography of critical articles on Baratynskii.

FRIZMAN, L. G. *Tvorcheskii put' Baratynskogo (Baratynskii's Creative Path)*. Moscow: Nauka, 1966. A book-length work with tedious emphasis on the social aspects of Baratynskii's verse.

————. "V. Ia. Briusov—issledovatel' E. A. Baratynskogo" ("V.

Ia. Briusov—Researcher of E. A. Baratynskii"), *Russkaia litera-tura (Russian Literature)*, No. 1 (1967). Survey of Briusov's articles, published and unpublished, on Baratynskii.

————."Zapadnye issledovateli Baratynskogo" ("Western Re-searchers of Baratynskii"), *Voprosy literatury (Problems of Literature)*, No. 2 (1964). A partial survey written from a nega-tive point of view

GALAKHOV, A. D. "E. A. Baratynskii," *Otechestvennye zapiski (Notes of the Fatherland)*, XXXVII (1844). Concerned with Baratynskii's poetic thought; repeats the basic position of Belinskii's 1842 article.

GINSBURG, L. "Lirika Baratynskogo" ("Baratynskii's Lyrics"), *Russkaia literatura (Russian Literature)*, No. 2 (1964). A sound essay on Baratynskii's poetic techniques and methods.

GOFMAN, M. L. "Baratynskii o Pushkine" ("Baratynskii on Push-kin"), *Pushkin i ego sovremenniki (Pushkin and His Contem-poraries)*, No. 16. St. Petersburg, 1913. On the relationship between the two poets.

————"Batiushkov i Boratynskii" ("Batiushkov and Bora-tynskii"), *Pravitel'stvennyi vestnik (Governmental Bulletin)*, No. 98 (1914). On the interrelationships in the work of the two poets.

————. "Lirika B-go" ("B-ii's Lyrics"), *Russkaia starina (Russian Antiquities)*, Vol. 158, Vol. 159 (1914). Deals with literary influences and general characteristics of Baratynskii's verse.

————. "Poemy B-go" ("B-ii's Long Poems"), *Russkaia starina (Russian Antiquities)*, Vol. 161. (1915). Examination of the long poems with emphasis on their Realistic tendencies.

————. *Poeziia Boratynskogo; istoriko-literaturnyi etiud' (Bora-tynskii's Poetry; an Historical-Literary Study)*. Petrograd: Gos. Tipografiia, 1915. An interesting study of influences and tech-niques.

IAZYKOV, D. D. *Evgenii Abramovich Baratynskii.* Moscow: Univ. Tipografiia, 1894. A brief biography.

ILESHIN, BORIS I. *Poet Evgenii Abramovich Boratynskii (The Poet Evgenii Abramovich Boratynskii)*. Tambov: Tambovskoe knizh-noe delo, 1961. Brief biography.

IVASK, IURII. "Boratynskii," *Novyi zhurnal (New Review)*, L (1957). An engaging discussion of various aspects of Baratynskii's work and biography.

KICHEEV, PETR. "Eshche neskol'ko slov o E. A. B-om ("A Few

More Words about E. A. B-ii''), *Russkii arkhiv (Russian Archives)*, No. 6 (1868). A short, but fascinating memoir.

KIREEVSKII, I. V. "Obozrenie russkoi slovesnosti za 1829 g." ("Review of Russian Literature for 1829"), *Polnoe sobranie sochinenii (Complete Works)*, Vol. II. Moscow: Tipografiia Imperatorskogo Moskovskogo Universiteta, 1911. A discerning commentary on the character of Baratynskii's poetic inspiration, and, in particular, on "The Ball."

————. "Obozrenie russkoi slovesnosti za 1831 g." ("Review of Russian Literature for 1831"), *Polnoe sobranie sochinenii (Complete Works)*, Vol. II. Moscow: Tipografiia Imperatorskogo Moskovskogo Universiteta, 1911. Includes penetrating remarks on Baratynskii's poetry, especially on "The Gypsy Girl."

KOTLIAREVSKII, N. A. "Zvezda razroznennoi Pleiady" ("Star of Pleiad Set Asunder"), *Starinnye portrety (Antique Portraits)*. St. Petersburg: Tipografiia M. M. Stansiulevicha, 1907. A lengthy treatise on Baratynskii's poetry against the background of literary trends of the time.

KUPREIANOVA, E. N. "Baratynskii," *Istoriia russkoi literatury (History of Russian Literature)*, Vol. VI. Moscow: Akademiia Nauk SSSR, 1953. A not uninteresting article characterized largely by the attempt to explain the nature of Baratynskii's poetry by political and ideological trends of the 1820's and 1830's.

————. "Esteticheskie vzgliady Baratynskogo" ("Baratynskii's Esthetic Views"), *Literaturnaia ucheba (Literary Studies)*, No. II (1936). A useful discussion of Baratynskii's creative development.

LONGINOV, M. "Baratynskii i ego sochineniia" ("Baratynskii and His Works"), *Russkii arkhiv (Russian Archives)*, No. 2 (1867). Contains absorbing details and comments on Baratynskii's life and poetry.

MAKSIMOV, N. "E. A. Baratynskii po bumagam Pazheskogo E. I. V. Korpusa" ("E. A. Baratynskii in the Papers of H. I. M. Pages' Corps"), *Russkaia starina (Russian Antiquities)*, Vol. II (1870). Documents Baratynskii's years at the Corps.

MALKINA, E. "Finliandskaia povest' Baratynskogo" ("Baratynskii's Tale of Finland"), *Literaturnaia ucheba (Literary Studies)*, No. 2 (1939). Excellent study of "Eda" in connection both with literary polemics of the early 1820's and with Pushkin's "The Captive of the Caucasus."

MAZEPA, N. R. *E. A. Baratynskii. Esteticheskie i literaturno-kriticheskie vzgliady (E. A. Baratynskii. Esthetic and Liter-ary-Critical Views).* Kiev: Akademiia Nauk SSSR, 1960. A detailed examination of Baratynskii's work, including his critical and creative thought.

MIRSKY, D. S. "Baratynsky," *A History of Russian Literature from its Beginnings to 1900,* ed. Francis J. Whitfield. New York: Vintage, 1961. Brief article on the survey level.

MURAV'EV, V. "Baratynskii i pushkinskaia pleiada" ("Baratynskii and the Pushkin Pleiad"), *Nastuplenia (Attack),* No. 2 (1935). Interesting essay on Baratynskii's poetry, with emphasis on its Romantic, irrational aspects.

NADEZHDIN, N. I. "Dve povesti v stikhakh: 'Bal' i 'Graf Nulin' " ("Two Tales in Verse: 'The Ball' and 'Count Nulin' "), *Vestnik Evropy (Herald of Europe),* No. 2 (1829). Negative criticism.

———. " 'Nalozhnitsa,' sochinenie E. Baratynskogo" (" 'The Concubine,' a Work of E. Baratynskii"), *Teleskop (Telescope),* No. 10 (1831). Negative in viewpoint, attacks, in particular, the ideas in the preface of the poem.

NECHAEVA, V. S. "Iz arkhiva Boratynskogo (From Boratynskii's Archives"), *Utrenniki (Morning Frosts),* Vol. 1. Petrograd, 1922. Specialized article concerned with certain of Baratynskii's changes in "Eda" and "Feasts," as well as the tracing of selected images in the latter from Viazemskii to Pushkin.

ORLOV, V. "E. A. Baratynskii," *Ocherki po istorii russkoi litera-tury pervoi poloviny XIX veka (Essays on the History of Russian Literature of the First Half of the XIX Century),* No. 1. Baku, 1941. A general discussion.

PLETNEV, P. A. "E. A. Baratynskii," *Sochineniia i perepiska (Works and Correspondence),* Vol. I. St. Petersburg: Ia. Grot, 1885. One of the few articles to defend Baratynskii after his death.

———. "O stikhotvoreniiakh Baratynskogo" ("On Baratynskii's Poems"), *Severnye tsvety na 1828 god (Northern Flowers for 1828).* St. Petersburg, 1827. Positive review of Baratynskii's 1827 collection.

———. "Pis'mo k Grafine S. I. S. o russkikh poetakh" ("Letter to Countess S. I. S. on Russian Poets"), *Sochineniia i perepiska (Works and Correspondence),* Vol. I. St. Petersburg: Ia. Grot, 1885. Notes on the characteristics of Baratynskii's elegiacal verse.

PUSHKIN, A. S. " 'Bal' Baratynskogo" ("Baratynskii's 'The Ball' "), *Polnoe sobranie sochinenii v desiati tomakh (Complete Works in*

Ten Volumes), 3rd edition, Vol. VII. Moscow: Akademiia Nauk SSSR, 1964. Positive, but unfinished review of "The Ball."

————. "Baratynskii," *Polnoe sobranie sochinenii v desiati tomakh (Complete Works in Ten Volumes)*, 3rd edition, Vol. VII. Moscow: Akademiia Nauk SSSR, 1964. Attempts to explain the reasons for Baratynskii's loss of popularity and has penetrating comments on his verse; unfinished.

————. "Stikhotvoreniia Evgeniia Baratynskogo 1827 g." ("Evgenii Baratynskii's Poems of 1827"), *Polnoe sobranie sochinenii v desiati tomakh (Complete Works in Ten Volumes)*, 3rd edition, Vol. VII. Moscow: Akademiia Nauk SSSR, 1964. Brief, unfinished review.

PYPIN, A. N. "Baratynskii," *Istoriia russkoi literatury (History of Russian Literature)*, 3rd edition, Vol. IV. St. Petersburg: Tipografiia M. M. Stansiulevicha, 1907. Reproaches Baratynskii for failure to understand his times.

SAVODNIK, V. F. "E. A. Baratynskii," *Russkii vestnik (Russian Herald)*, No. 4 (April, 1900), No. 5 (May, 1900). Critical examination of Baratynskii's poetic thought and ideas.

SEMENOV, LEONID. "Lermontov i Boratynskii" ("Lermontov and Boratynskii"), *M. Iu. Lermontov*. Moscow: N. P. Karabasnikov, 1915. Points out certain similarities in the work of these poets.

SETSCHKAREFF, W. "Zur philosophischen Lyrik Boratynskijs," *Zeitschrift für Slavische Philologie*, XIX, 2 (1947). Emphasizes Schelling's influence on the development of Baratynskii's poetry.

STOROZHENKO, N. "Poet-myslitel'" ("The Poet-Thinker"), *Iz oblasti literatury (From the Literary Sphere)*. Moscow: Tipo-lit. A. V. Vasil'eva i ko., 1902. Brief comments on various aspects of Baratynskii's life and poetry.

STRUVE, GLEB. "Evgeny Baratynsky," *The Slavonic and East European Review*, Vol. XXIII (January, 1945). Useful article on Baratynskii's poetry and poetic development.

VENGEROV, S. "Baratynskii," *Kritiko-biograficheskii slovar' russkikh pisatelei i uchenykh (Critical-Biographical Dictionary of Russian Writers and Scholars*, Vol. II. St. Petersburg: A. Efron, 1891. Concentrates on the indecisive nature of Baratynskii's verse.

VERKHOVSKII, IU. "O simvolizme Baratynskogo" ("On Baratynskii's Symbolism"), *Trudy i dni (Works and Days)*, No. 3 (1912).

Discusses Baratynskii's verse in connection with Symbolist criteria, emphasizes its antithetical qualities.

VIAZEMSKII, P. A. "Baratynskii," *Polnoe sobranie sochinenii (Complete Works)*, Vol. VII. St. Petersburg: S. D. Sheremetev, 1882. Written on the appearance of Baratynskii's *Works* in 1869.

————. "Staraia zapisnaia knizhka" ("Old Note-book"), *Polnoe sobranie sochinenii (Complete Works)*, Vol. VIII. St. Petersburg: S. D. Sheremetev, 1883. A note on Baratynskii's poetic intellect.

ZHURAKOVSKII, E. "Poet-pessimist i blizhaishii sputnik poezii Pushkina" ("The Poet-Pessimist and Close Fellow Traveler of Pushkin's Poetry"), *Simptomy literaturnoi evoliutsii (Symptoms of Literary Evolution)*, Moscow: Tipo-lit. M. M. Tarchigina, 1903. A lengthy article on Baratynskii in connection with commentary on Pushkin's poetry.

Index